Early Decorative

Textiles

Early Decorative Textiles

Textiles

W. Fritz Volbach

Paul Hamlyn

LONDON · NEW YORK · SYDNEY · TORONTO

Translated by Yuri Gabriel from the Italian original

Il Tessuto nell'Arte Antica

1966 Fratelli Fabbri Editori, Milan

This edition © 1969
The Hamlyn Publishing Group Limited
Hamlyn House,
The Centre, Feltham,
Middlesex

Text filmset in Great Britain by Keyspools Ltd,
Golborne

Printed in Italy by Fratelli Fabbri Editori,
Milan

Weaving is almost as old as man himself. Man differs from animals in that he walks upright and, being endowed with a capacity for abstract thought, is able to make tools to help him in his quest for food and shelter. Man alone can control fire, and he alone discovered that clothing could protect him from both heat and cold.

The Bible refers to this development when it describes how Adam and Eve made themselves aprons of fig-leaves after the Fall, and how they were expelled from the Garden of Eden wearing 'coats of skins'. To what extent this was the result of moral rather than practical considerations is an open question. The 'clothes' themselves must have been similar to those worn by hunter peoples like Indians and Eskimos. A considerable number of bone needles have been found in France: those of the Aurignacian culture have no eyes, but eyes already occur in Magdalenian needles. In contrast to the hunter cultures, those of the Mesolithic period saw a development in the type of clothing worn and the technique of its manufacture. The sedentary peasant population now had plants as well as animals to provide them with raw materials for their textiles. Mats covered the floors of the huts and hangings were draped in front of the doorways or decorated the walls. What clothes looked like is not known for certain, but, as in the Bronze Age, they may have been made of linen, like the fragments of plaited and woven cloth—dating from as early as the 3rd millennium BC—which have been found in several localities, including Egypt and the lake dwellings of Switzerland.

Materials in which simple weaving and rich patterns are combined represent a considerable degree of development. Patterned textiles in which the basic weave has been supplemented by inlaid weft threads have been found in Egypt, dating from the 22nd Dynasty (945–745 BC). For a while strips of bast, hide and similar materials were used, mainly for plaiting, but soon the need was felt for a more uniform material, a twisted thread prepared with the aid of the kind of distaff one can still see in use in many countries today. Where and when this discovery was made remains a mystery, but in the Middle Ages spinning was invariably associated with Eve. The loom and all its accessories was certainly already in use in the late Stone Age.

Egyptian reliefs and wall-paintings, like those at Beni-Hasan (2380–2167 BC), show what the earliest primitive horizontal looms looked like. The vertical loom made its appearance during the New Kingdom. The warp then lay either vertically or horizontally, and the fabric was opened with a batten until it was discovered that this could be done by connecting the beams of the loom with pedals operated by the weaver. This meant that the weaver could use both hands to manipulate the shuttle.

For the most part, plain linen cloth of the kind generally used to bind mummies was produced, but Egyptian wall-paintings prove that patterned stuffs must also have been woven. The tomb of Pharaoh Tuthmosis II (*c.* 1400 BC) certainly contained cloth with a papyrus and lotus blossom design, though it is possible that the design was embroidered or even painted on.

Though Egyptian paintings have made an important contribution to the study of the development of weaving techniques, other Mediterranean countries, above all Greece and the kingdoms of the Near East, have provided such a wealth of written sources that the first flowering of the art of weaving must surely be sought there. Unfortunately none of the fabrics themselves have yet been found, but carved reliefs demonstrate the importance the Babylonians and Assyrians attached to wall-hangings and rich clothing. In the *Iliad* Homer speaks enthusiastically of 'Babylonian cloths', and it is very likely that these '*babylonica peristromata*' are the same as the wall-hangings and fabrics to which Pliny refers and for which Nero and Scipio paid Roman art-dealers such

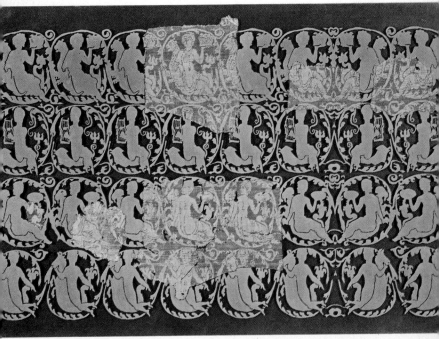

1. Nereids riding sea-monsters. Fragments of four rows.
Silk twill. 4th–5th century. Sion Cathedral treasure.

2. Nilotic scene. Decorative panel. *c.* 5th century. Louvre, Paris. (Photo: Giradon)

1.   Nereids riding sea monsters. Fragments of four rows. Silk twill. 4th–5th century. Sion Cathedral treasure. Formerly used as a reliquary cloth. There are other fragments in the Berlin and Zürich museums. Similar motifs in Alexandrian bone carvings suggest that the cloth may have been made in Egypt. There are related fabrics with maenads in Sens, with horses in St Maurice d'Agaune, and in Rimini.

2.   Nilotic scene. Decorative panel. Wool on linen. *c.* 5th century. Louvre, Paris. Pagan motifs were frequently used by Coptic weavers, who developed them according to their own taste. The design includes children, nereids, fishermen, ducks, fish and lotus flowers. (Photo: Giradon).

3.   Fish. Fragment of a wall-hanging or cover. Wool on linen. Egyptian, from Antinoë; excavated by Gayet. About the 3rd century. Previously in the Musée Guimet, now in the Musée du Louvre, Paris. There is an identical piece in the textile museum in Lyons. Still completely in the classical spirit, and realistic, as the shadows under the fish indicate. Very reminiscent of frescoes and mosaic floors like those in Aquileia Cathedral. Judging from the evidence of the *Liber de caeremoniis*, this motif persisted until the Middle Ages.

4.   Two nereids; borders with birds. Length 1·43 m. Wool on linen. Egyptian, from Akhmim; 4th century. Collection Dumbarton Oaks, Washington. The nereid on the bull-like animal might represent Europa with Jupiter, the other with the mirror perhaps Venus. Related to Egyptian wool-embroidered fabrics. Similar motifs are found in contemporary sculpture: reliefs from Ahnas in the Coptic Museum in Cairo or from Oxyrhynchus in the Alexandria Museum.

3. Fish. Fragment of a wall-hanging or cover.

4. Two nereids. Wool on linen. Egyptian, 4th century.
Collection Dumbarton Oaks, Washington.

fantastic prices. However, neither written nor pictorial sources give a clear indication of the techniques used. The larger wall-hangings with their historical or mythological scenes may have been entirely woven, but it is also possible that they were composed, to a greater or lesser extent, of small pieces of appliqué embroidery. Pliny, taking the latter view, thought Alexandrian cloth, which was woven in separate colours, represented an advance on the Babylonian: *'mal polymata appellant'*.

Apart from wool and linen, the Assyrians of the 7th and 6th centuries BC were also familiar with silk, and probably obtained some of their supplies from silkworms. Cotton is mentioned by Herodotus. To what extent it was imported from India, or silk from China, remains uncertain; but what is known is that Indian cotton did not reach Greece until the time of Alexander the Great.

Ornamental motifs based on creatures of fable—sphinxes, birds, mountain goats, bulls, etc.—which more often than not originated from Nineveh, now began to make their appearance. Indeed, this bestiary remained an important element in the artistic vocabulary of the Mediterranean region until towards the end of the Middle Ages. Symbolic beasts copied from Eastern fabrics also played a decisive role in architectural sculpture in Italy, France and Spain, and the lion, the eagle and the elephant, all symbols of sovereignty, were the main motifs in the court art of Byzantium.

If one looks at the oldest types of cloth shown in

Greek vase paintings, one cannot fail to see how closely related they are to earlier Eastern materials. The diagonal stripes on the clothes shown on the François vase in Florence are clearly related to Near Eastern originals, and the decorative bands with winged horses, griffons and Gorgons on the loom behind Penelope in a 5th-century red-figure vase from Chiusi are quite evidently in the same tradition. The loom itself is scarcely distinguishable from Egyptian looms of the same period. But from now on the Near Eastern style of decoration was used only when portraying Asiatics, as in the mosaic (now in Naples) of Alexander at the Battle of Issus. Pliny also speaks of a transparent material for women's clothes (*ut denudet feminas vestis*) imported from Cos.

The caravan route that brought raw silk from China to the borders of Persia and Bactria had been operating since 114 BC, and about this time too the use of gold thread was gradually becoming established. Fortunately a number of rich and colourful costume fabrics, most of them found near the Kerch road in the Crimea, have survived; the bulk of the collection is now in the Hermitage Museum in Leningrad. The designs, with tendrils, acanthus leaves, and ducks and stags' heads worked in wool, illustrate the Hellenistic style of the 4th–3rd centuries BC.

As Rome grew in wealth and its empire spread—as far as the Euphrates in the East—so too the demand for expensive materials, above all for imported silk, increased. A vain attempt to make clothes less lavish was made in the century before the beginning of the

Christian era, and in the centuries that followed there were repeated complaints about, and even proclamations against, this form of extravagance.

The systematic cultivation of silk began in China during the reign of the Empress Hsi Ling Shi, and under the Han dynasty the raw material, as well as made-up cloth, was being sent to the West in increasing quantities. Specimens of silk cloth were found in Palmyra, which means they must have reached there before 272 BC, when the city was destroyed. As a result of various finds made by Aurel Stein at Jarin Bechen and Loulan, the route the silk caravans took across Central Asia from the 2nd century BC onwards is now known, even though no actual costume fabrics have been discovered. A second important find was made by Kozlov and Borovka in the Noin-Ula Mountains in Mongolia, and fabrics of the same kind came to light in Syria and Doura-Europos.

The chief centres of the silk industry developed at the western end of the caravan route, in towns like Tyre and Berytus (Beirut) which had the additional advantage over smaller centres of being in a position to dye the silk with real purple. It was only after the introduction of sericulture in the reign of Justinian that Constantinople was able to compete with these markets.

Silk was apparently still very expensive in Rome, for Lucian and Pliny record that women there unravelled heavy silk cloth and remade it into lighter fabrics. Caligula was thought slightly eccentric for wearing a silk chlamys, but when the Syrian Emperor

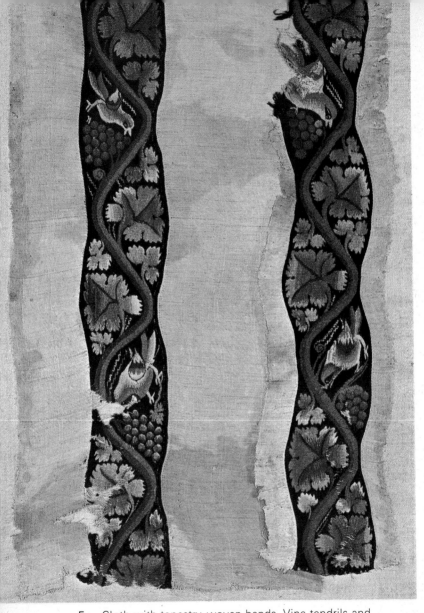

5.   Cloth with tapestry-woven bands. Vine tendrils and
birds. Wool on linen. Egyptian, 3rd—4th century. Victoria and
Albert Museum, London.

6. Peacock. Rectangular panel. Wool on linen. Wide linen surround of looped weave. Egyptian, 4th century. Staatliche Museen, Berlin.

5.   Cloth with tapestry-woven bands with a design of vine tendrils and birds. Wool on linen. Egyptian, 3rd–4th century. Victoria and Albert Museum, London. There are related bands with similar Hellenistic designs and colours in, for example, Berlin.

6.   Peacock. Rectangular panel. Wool on linen. Wide linen surround of looped weave. Egyptian, 4th century. Staatliche Museen, Berlin. There are related realistic animal subjects in Brussels and elsewhere. The panel is reminiscent of early designs like those in catacombs in Rome and Cyrene, but this particular design definitely does not have a Christian significance.

7.   Head of Dionysus. One of a pair: in the other the head is looking in the opposite direction. Linen and wool. Egyptian, 3rd–4th century. Textile Museum, Washington. The garland of vine leaves in the hair identifies it as Dionysus. Still completely Hellenistic in style; very similar to the female head in Detroit (plate 10).

7. Head of Dionysus.

Heliogabalus dressed himself completely in silk he was considered positively effeminate. These types of silk were called *holoserica, tramaserica* and *subserica* because the Chinese were known as *Seres* and silk was named *serica* after them. Even under Aurelian (died AD 275) silk was so expensive that he refused to buy his wife a purple silk cloak, and in AD 301 Diocletian issued an edict fixing the price of the raw material at 4,000 gold pieces a kilo. Numerous paintings and mosaics, like those in the Piazza Armerina in Sicily, show garments covered with decorative panels and appliqué work, but hardly any of them have survived. One of the most important fragments, a *Nike* in gold, comes from Kostolats, the Viminacium of antiquity, and is an example of the type of bullion work described by Pliny. The theory that this technique was used for ceremonial clothing in the 4th century is substantiated by the small fragment in the Victoria and Albert Museum in London, and also by the golden bands in the Salonika Museum, which may perhaps date from a somewhat later period.

Some of the fragments of silk cloth used to wrap round holy relics date from the early Hellenistic period, and lay undiscovered until modern times in church treasures in Sens, Aachen, Trier, St Maurice, Sion and even Rome. One of the earliest, a material with a maenad motif at Sion, is 5th-century in style, as are the fragments of cloth from the tomb of St Julian in Rimini. The maenad cloth at Sens appears to be somewhat later, but is still based on a Greek original. The same applies to another fabric at Sens, one with griffons and ducks on a yellow ground; it is reminiscent of the Hellenistic duck fabric in Leningrad.

Obviously these materials could be used for any purpose, for wall-hangings as well as clothes. Giovanni Crisostomo (*c.* 345–407) and particularly Asterio of Amasia (died *c.* 410) pronounced against them. The latter, indeed, objected to all clothes with pictorial representations, and not only those with huntsmen, forests, bears and bulls, but also those with scenes from the scriptures, even miracles. The small Boston fragment with a shepherd and his sheep is an example of the last category. Some indication of the vast number of such garments in existence at that time is given by the fact that in 409 Alaric demanded 4,000 silk tunics from Rome. According to Ammianus Marcellinus (339–400) even the masses wore them.

Byzantium, which Constantine the Great chose as his capital in AD 330, became in due course one of the main centres for the production and distribution of cloth. As a result, links with Eastern manufacturers became ever stronger, as did those of Rome with the western half of the Empire. Cloth was woven in the women's quarters of the imperial palace, and part of the output was reserved for the emperor himself and his chief officials. The dyers, gold-embroiderers and tailors were so tied to their work that before they could stop for even a moment they had to find someone to take their place.

In 369 Valens and Valentinian issued a decree granting Constantinople the sole right to manufacture gold and silk lace like that found in Thessalonica. In 424 Theodosius II banned the production of purple silk by private enterprise. Again it is only possible to get an idea of these rich fabrics at second hand, from the mosaics in Hagios Georgios in Thessalonica or from ivory consular diptychs. Small rosettes and palmettes were a favourite motif, but a Byzantine origin cannot be certainly ascribed to the small fragments of asymmetrically patterned material in Aachen, Rome and Sens.

The industry reached its peak under Justinian I, when two monks returning from China brought him silkworm eggs hidden in a stick. As a result, Byzantium was able to free itself from the enormous cost of transporting the material and the high duties levied by the Persians. For the first time Byzantine silk could compete with the Eastern variety in the export market. This also affected politics, for a gift of silk to a foreign ruler was a mark of special favour. And, naturally, smuggling also prospered.

Though Syrian cloths, for example those found by Pfister at Doura-Europos, Palmyra and Halabjah (the Zenobia of antiquity), provide examples of a wider range of techniques, the finds made in Egyptian tombs are both richer and more important as far as our overall knowledge of ancient textiles is concerned. Here the warm dry desert sand preserved thousands upon thousands of pieces of cloth dating from the 2nd century onwards (the 2nd century saw the end of the practice of mummification), including many from the period after the Arab conquest (640).

8.   Tapestry-woven panel of a hare. Wool and linen.
Egyptian, 3rd–4th century. Musée Historique des Tissus,
Lyons

9. Nereid. Square panel. Wool on linen. Egyptian, 3rd—4th century. Museum of Arts, Cleveland.

10. Female head. Fragment. Wool on linen. Egyptian, 3rd–4th century. Institute of Arts, Detroit.

8.   Hare. Rectangular tapestry-woven panel. Wool and linen. Multicoloured border within a surround of natural-coloured, long-threaded looped weave. Egyptian, from Faiyûm; 3rd–4th century. Musée Historique des Tissus, Lyons. A hare nibbling at a bunch of grapes was a favourite motif: there are similar items from Akhmim in London, Moscow, Berlin, New York and the Bouvier Collection in Switzerland.

9.   Nereid. Square panel. Border with vines and birds. Wool on linen. Egyptian, 3rd–4th century. Museum of Art, Cleveland. Woman, probably a nereid, wearing a diadem and a necklace with a pendant. Similar to the large figure of a female dancer formerly in Berlin and to the figure in the Dumbarton Oaks Collection (plate 4). The plastic treatment of the body suggests a date of origin somewhere in the 3rd or 4th century.

10.   Female head. Fragment. Wool on linen. Egyptian, 3rd–4th century. Institute of Arts, Detroit. There are earrings and a diadem in the piled-up hair and a nimbus behind the head, which is naturalistically represented and looks to the left. The expressiveness of the design is reminiscent of late portraits from Faiyûm.

11.   Orante. Fragment, probably of a curtain. Height 69·8 cm. Wool on linen. Looped weave. Egyptian, from Schech Sayet; 5th century. Institute of Arts, Detroit. The subject is probably a female orante; she wears a necklace and a red tunic with a maphorion, and is shown standing under an arch. On either side of her are vases with flowers. The attitude of the figure suggests that this is a Christian subject. Perhaps it is part of a large curtain like the one found in the infant burial in Schech Abade, now in a private collection in Munich. The motif is already Coptic in its rigid frontality.

11. Orante. Fragment, probably of a curtain.

Fragments of clothing were the most common finds in the graves along the whole length of the Nile valley, as well as in oases like Kargeh. But sometimes, as in the recent excavation of the mass grave of children at Antinoë, the finds included large hangings and the kind of coverings spread over the bodies of dead people of importance. All these sites have been ransacked, and the activities of grave-robbers have made it almost impossible to make exact observations. Indeed, no excavation has yet been made using modern methods. Regrettably, even large museums like Paris, Lyons and Berlin were more concerned with finding textiles that were decorative or valuable than with the careful observation and documentation that would have given them a basis for dating.

The sites themselves generally lie near old towns or the large monasteries behind the agricultural belt—which, as farmland, was too valuable to waste. As yet, unfortunately, no Alexandrian fabrics have been discovered and most 'Alexandrian silk' is so named without justification. Very few finds have been made in the Nile delta or near Cairo, though some beautiful Islamic silks came to light at Fostat. Faiyûm, however, proved more rewarding, and good finds were made at Crocodilopolis.

Antinoë, an elegant city and one of the main centres of government, and the more modest town of Akhmim (Panopolis), provided the richest and most numerous finds. But the excavations at Karanis, Hawara and in the neighbourhood of the monastery of Sakkara were less fruitful. A study of these fabrics reveals that each town had its own workshop, and the quality of the fabrics varied with the social status of the customer. Consequently the best work from the point of view of both style and technique was found at Antinoë, a rich Hellenistic city with a highly-developed culture and numerous government officials among its inhabitants. But the finds also included quantities of textiles probably imported for the various non-Egyptian communities such as the Persians and Byzantines. Among the materials were batik prints, proof of the existence of communication with India, and large wall-hangings and coverings (plate 3) printed with scenes from antiquity, for example the story of Dionysus, or with such Christian subjects as Moses or St Peter. Only two colours were used for the hangings which, although made in Egypt, have close stylistic affinities with Roman work. The imperial style imposed itself even on Egypt—with its conglomeration of different cultures—until, in the 5th century, a new, more genuinely local style (the 'Coptic') developed as a result of a newly-awakened national consciousness.

Interest in this form of art is nothing new. As early as the 17th century a nobleman by the name of Wieckmann (1617–1681) was collecting textiles of this period, albeit as curios. His collection is now in the Ulm Museum. Napoleon's archaeologists also became interested in the subject during the period of French occupation (1798–1801) and they bequeathed their finds to the Turin Museum. But it was only in the 19th century, after Maspero had discovered (1884) the burial grounds near Akhmim, that European museums began to build up collections of these fabrics systematically. Foremost among the collectors were textile museums which needed the fabrics to illustrate the development of weaving. Theodor Graf carried out excavations in Sakkara for Vienna, Wladimir de Bock in Faiyûm and Akhmim for St Petersburg, André Gayet in Antinoë for Lyons and Paris, Robert Forrer in Akhmim, Carl Schmidt in Antinoë for Berlin, and after him Salmi for Florence. The American museums did not arrive on the scene till the 20th century when, with large sums of money at their disposal, they bought selected items, mainly from art dealers, for their collections in Washington, Cleveland, New York and Boston.

In this mass of materials there is not one that can definitely be dated. The best that has been done so far is to fix a date between 454 and 456 to a large curtain (plate 30) now in Brussels. It came from Antinoë and has two busts in the top half—perhaps Aurelius Colluthus and his wife Tisoia. Papyri found with the curtain provided the date, which agrees with dates attributed to similar fabrics on purely stylistic grounds.

Various museums have published catalogues of their fabric collections. Among the authors of these catalogues are: Karabacek (Vienna); A. F. Kendrick (London); O. Wulff and W. F. Volbach (Berlin); J. Errera (Brussels); A. Apostolaki (Athens); W. M. Wilson (Ann Arbor); M. Matye and K. Liapunova

12. Orante. Fragment, probably of a wall-hanging. Wool on linen. Egyptian, 4th–5th century. Textile Museum, Washington.

13. The Sacrifice of Isaac. Egyptian, 4th–5th century. Cooper Union Museum, New York.

14. Head in surround decorated with vine stems. Rectangular panel. Wool on linen. Egyptian, 4th–5th century. Muséum für angewandte Kunst, Vienna.

15. Head in a surround decorated with vine stems. Rectangular panel. Wool on linen. Egyptian, 4th–5th century. Collection Bérard, Paris.

12. Orante. Fragment, probably of a wall-hanging. Wool on linen. Looped weave. Egyptian, 4th–5th century. Textile Museum, Washington. The man, a saint or a priest, wears a tunic decorated with a cruciform design and stands between two tall candlesticks (the left one is missing). Between the candlestick and the nimbus round his head are two letters. The technique employed links the fragment with earlier looped weaves, but there is a considerable degree of rigidity and stylisation in the design. There is a similar piece from Akhmim in London.

13. The sacrifice of Isaac. Egyptian, 4th–5th century. Cooper Union Museum, New York. Photo: Francis G. Mayer. Fragment with a powerful, fluid representation of a Biblical scene and a decorative pattern based on familiar motifs.

14. Head in a surround decorated with vine stems. Rectangular panel. Wool on linen. Egyptian, from Akhmim; 4th–5th century. Museum für angewandte Kunst, Vienna. The head looks to the left, but in all other respects it is identical with the specimen reproduced in plate 15.

15. Head in a surround decorated with vine stems. Rectangular panel. Wool on linen. Egyptian, from Akhmim; 4th–5th century. Collection Bérard, Paris. The male head, the vine leaves and the grapes are all still relatively realistic in style. This and the almost identical piece in plate 14 probably formed a matching pair.

16. Decorative panel. Wool on linen. Egyptian, from Akhmim; 5th century. Collection Bérard, Paris. Four vine leaves in a cruciform design are centred on a small square containing a male head. Christian symbolism has been imputed to this design.

16. Decorative panel. Wool on linen.

(Moscow and Leningrad); W. F. Volbach (Mainz and the Vatican); P. du Bourguet (Louvre).

The 'Coptic Art' exhibition held in Essen in 1963 was a great step forward because it meant that experts like John Beckwith, Geza de Francovich and Pierre du Bourguet were making concerted efforts to provide a more exact system of dating. The attempts of Professor Geza de Francovich of Rome to throw light on the whole question by comparing the development of weaving with that of Coptic painting and sculpture have been of the greatest importance. But even here, despite the work of men like Strzygowski, George Duthuit, Monnier and de Villard, and Kitzinger, areas of uncertainty remain.

Though the method of stylistic comparison has clarified the picture considerably, it must be remembered that speed of stylistic development varied with place: styles developed much more slowly in small towns than, for instance, in Antinoë, where the various manufacturers could see for themselves the latest fashions from all over the kingdom. By being able to date roughly fabrics found in Palmyra, for example the purple tunic with a geometrical design which must have been made before the town was destroyed in 273 BC, we can recognise the early, still Hellenistic phase elsewhere: in Antinoë, for instance, which was founded by the Emperor Hadrian in AD 130 for his favourite, Antinoüs.

Attempts have been made, by Pfister in particular, to work out a new system of classification by means of chemical tests or by comparative analysis of technical characteristics. It is hoped that these will achieve greater accuracy in dating, but such experiments have not so far proved entirely satisfactory. Pfister believed that the Syrian and Mesopotamian woollen cloths and the Indian cottons he studied were woven from the right (Z) and that Egyptian linen was woven from the left (S). Unfortunately, this theory does not hold for Near Eastern fabrics in general. And the value of the method by which the age of purple materials is determined—by subjecting them to dyes like madder—is still questionable.

Some of the oldest fabrics, to judge by style, are those woven in more than one colour, generally with subjects taken from antiquity. The materials used are wool and linen, and the designs are reminiscent of classical wall-paintings. Excellent examples of this are two decorative roundels, probably from a tunic, one (now in Leningrad) with the earth (Gea) in the form of Isis, the other (now in Moscow) with a personification of the Nile wearing a rich garland of flowers. They probably date from the 3rd or 4th century at the latest, since the design and colours are so impressionistic that it seems unlikely that they were copied from an earlier original. Similarly the portrait of a woman with a nimbus (plate 10) is reminiscent of 3rd-century mummy portraits. (These portraits, painted on panels, showed the facial characteristics of the dead person naturalistically and were placed over the face of the corpse, while the rest of the body was bandaged.) But the Dionysus in Washington (plate 7) is somewhat stylised.

A more naturalistic style is revealed in the tapestry panels with animal designs used to decorate monochrome fabrics, in particular in the peacock reproduced in plate 6 and the hare from Faiyûm (plate 8). Both have something in common with the paintings in the catacombs of Rome. One of the earliest coloured fabrics from Antinoë is, unfortunately, very badly damaged; but the fragments in Lyons (plate 3) and Paris (Louvre) clearly show its pattern of fish on a green background. This design is so naturalistic that the fish have even been given shadows. The extent to which it was still influenced by Hellenistic art is evident when it is compared with the mosaics from Daphne. The colours of the double-banded material with the design of vines and birds pecking at grapes (plate 5) have lasted remarkably well. They also represent a naturalism that is still purely Hellenistic in form.

The nereid fabric in the Dumbarton Oaks Collection (plate 4) shows what a large wall-hanging looked like, and its similarity to the female head in Detroit indicates that it too belongs to the early period. But stylisation was beginning to make its appearance, as in the Ahnas reliefs in Cairo, and the mannerist technique of these carvings is fully developed in the 'Sabina shawl' from Antinoë, part of which is in Paris and part in Lyons. The square central panel shows Apollo and Daphne, as do the Ahnas relief and one of the ivories in Ravenna. There is also a panel with Bellerophon and Chimaera, again copied from an older original.

17. Decorative panel. Wool on linen. Egyptian, 5th century.
Kunstgewerbe Museum, Hamburg.

17.   Decorative panel. Wool on linen. Egyptian, 5th century. Kunstgewerbe Museum, Hamburg. The design shows a surround of tendrils containing a hunting scene with an Oceanus mask in the centre. Two warriors, a female panther and a stag. There is a similar rectangular panel in the Bouvier Collection in Gruyère. Hunting scenes are often shown on these 'purple stuffs' but they seldom have such elegant surrounds.

18.   Vase with the Tree of Life. Panel. Wool on linen. Egyptian, 5th–6th century. Museum für angewandte Kunst, Vienna. A tree with birds in its branches rises from a short-based vase decorated with a tongue design. A favourite motif in both the classical and Hellenistic periods. It also occurs in several other Egyptian fabrics, for example those in the textile museum in Lyons.

19.   Venus and Adonis. Roundel with square surround. Wool on linen. Egyptian, 4th century. Collection E. Kofler-Truniger, Lucerne. Adonis in hunting costume on the left, Venus veiled and wearing a crown on the right. Used as a decorative border. It has all the delicacy of the Hellenistic style, and is based on a classical model, like numerous similar items in Paris, London and Berlin.

20.   Portrait of a man. Wool on linen. Egyptian, from Akhmim; 5th century. Collection Bérard, Paris. Head-and-shoulders portrait of a man with a nimbus. On the right, a heart on a blue ground. Its realism still recalls the late mummy portraits, but the bright colours are already very Coptic.

18. Vase with the Tree of Life.

19. Venus and Adonis. Roundel with square surround. Wool on linen. Egyptian, 4th century. Collection E. Kofler-Truniger, Lucerne.

20. Portrait of a man. Wool on linen. Egyptian, 5th century.
Collection Bérard, Paris.

To this group of early Hellenistic coloured fabrics belong the 'looped weaves', in which the woollen weft is raised in loops above the surface of the linen, as in towelling today. Their designs imitate the broad, loose outlines of wall-paintings like those at Bawait, and their subjects too are similar. The technique was widely used for large wall-hangings, curtains and cushions. These were found in almost all burials, and many museums, including Berlin, London, Boston, Athens, Paris and Washington, have specimens in their collections. The fragment in Washington (plate 12) is a good early example, and the female figure in Detroit (plate 11) is even more stylised.

Figures of this type, set in arcades, seem to have been a favourite subject for large curtains. One such curtain, now in a private collection in Munich, was pieced together from fragments found in the child burial at Schech Abade. Fragments in the Abegg Foundation in Berne, the Benaki Collection in Athens and the Debbane Collection in Rome are very similar. In the later ones the Coptic style tends to dominate: the colours are harsher and are juxtaposed without intermediate tones. The looped weave technique was also often used for smaller items in purple cloth, like pillow-cases decorated with swastikas or other simple patterns.

The great mass of simple purple or dark blue wool-on-linen fabrics that crop up in the inventory of every find belong to the early, Hellenistic period. In the same stylistic group there are also fabrics with figural designs, the earliest of which have realistic representations of mythological subjects (that is, the motifs of classical antiquity). Simple geometrical patterns, on the other hand, were mainly used to decorate clothing: they were woven on the *clavi* (the decorative bands which were used to embellish the rest of the costume), on the cuff-bands, and on the round or square decorative panels on the shoulders or the lower part of the tunic.

These fabrics with their designs in indigo-dyed wool—indigo gave them roughly the same colour as purple—may well have been among the earliest Egyptian textiles. As already noted, there was little difference between the decorative band and roundel from Palmyra and the early Egyptian ones from Akhmim or Antinoë. And since the former must have been woven before 273, textiles of this kind may be very old indeed. Sometimes other colours are found to have been added, and, in the case of particularly expensive materials, gold thread. This style was so popular that a Coptic adaptation of it lasted well into the Islamic period. Christian motifs were not used in the early textiles; they only start appearing after the 5th century. The usual motifs are simple geometrical patterns often based on leaves—for example the beautiful specimen from Akhmim, now in the Bérard Collection in Paris (plate 16), which has four leaves in the form of a cross centred on a man's head—or vases with leafy branches in which birds are nesting (plate 18). The Hamburg material with tendrils and hunting scenes (plate 17) is unusual in both subject and technique. The material in the

Bérard Collection has a square panel with an expressive head in the centre and a delicately stylised leaf on each of the four sides; it links this style with Hellenistic coloured fabrics. More examples could be given, but the importance lies in the figural designs.

The mythological scenes on some of these fabrics derive from ancient drama. Examples of this are a decorative roundel, still completely imbued with the spirit of antiquity, showing Venus with Adonis as a huntsman (plate 19); and the square panel of a shoulder ornament, now in Boston, with particularly finely worked nereids, tritons and cupids. This is woven in silk with a woollen weft (2), gold threads and woollen weft threads. Real purple (*burex brandaris*) was also used. Scenes of this kind, though not of this technical complexity, are fairly common. Examples are the Venus as the Goddess of Spring in the Bouvier Collection in Gruyère, the Phaedra and Hippolytus in Leningrad, the Judgment of Paris in Washington and Paris, Zeus and Hermes in Leningrad, Iphigenia with Orestes and Pylades in Frankfurt, Orpheus with animals in London, Hercules with Hippolytus in Athens, Hercules and the lion in Düsseldorf, and countless others on similar classical themes. And then there were putti, shepherds, women dancing, etc., taken from larger scenes. Most popular of all were the decorative panels, generally square in shape, with designs showing equestrian figures. These were often surrounded by nereids, sea-monsters and erotes—all thoroughly classical motifs.

Two main factors brought the naturalistic style favoured by antiquity to an end: the collapse of the Western Empire in the 5th century and a change in economic structure as a result of which a new social order was established and to which the language of art had to be adapted. The figures become more isolated and less mobile, and spatial depth is lost. The concept of 'Caesaropapism' which became firmly established under Justinian I in the middle of the 6th century, was the aspect of Byzantium that most affected the outside world. In Egypt, change was even more evident in the political field. The new 'nationalist' movement had close connections with the monks, whose power was steadily increasing. This movement returned to the roots of the old native culture and rejected the alien Hellenistic style of the 'court art' which had been introduced—mainly via Alexandria—by the Roman and Byzantine rulers. It is already evident in the architecture of Shenout's monastery near Sohag. The change in taste took some time to affect textiles, but the old classical motifs were gradually replaced by new subjects drawn from Eastern mythology, by portraits, and, above all, by Christian themes. Syrian silks, and Indian fabrics to some extent, and possibly also African art, had a strong influence on the creative imagination of the Coptic weavers.

In the art of the Eastern provinces too, local tendencies began to reassert themselves. Particularly strong links must have existed between Antinoë and Persia, since Gayet and Carl Schmidt found Persian

21. Sassanian royal device (senmurv). Silk twill. Sassanian, 6th–7th century. Victoria and Albert Museum, London.

22. Peacocks. Fragment of a reliquary cloth. Silk twill.
Iranian, 3rd–4th century. Aachen Cathedral treasure.

21.   Senmurv. Silk twill. From the reliquary of St Leu in Paris. Sassanian, 6th–7th century. Victoria and Albert Museum, London. The senmurv—like a fish of the hippocampus type— was one of the most important Sassanian royal devices and it remained in constant use not only in the post-Sassanian period, but also in Byzantine fabrics. The motif also occurs in the cliff reliefs at Taki Bostan (457–459/483) and in silver reliefs. There is a second piece in the Musée des Arts Décoratifs, Paris.

22.   Peacocks. Fragment of a reliquary cloth. Silk twill. Iranian, 3rd–4th century. Aachen Cathedral treasure. Pairs of confronting peacocks share a nimbus, above them lily-like leaves; between the peacocks, pillars with foliate capitals. Close in style to the Antinoë silks, this fabric is one of the best examples of its kind.

23.   Pheasant. Fragment in a rather poor state of preservation. Silk twill. From a reliquary in the Sancta Sanctorum in the Lateran in Rome. Sassanian, 4th century. Museo Sacro, Vatican. One of the few surviving Sassanian silks. Similar fabrics, like the hippocampus material in London, were used as models for later silks, particularly in Byzantium. The material with a cock pattern in the Vatican (plate 24) also comes into this group.

24.   Cock. Silk twill in superb condition. From a reliquary in the Sancta Sanctorum. Sassanian, 6th–7th century. Museo Sacro, Vatican. The cock has a nimbus and faces left. Between the surrounds are palmette motifs. In colour this fabric is close to the Vatican pheasant material, but its design is reminiscent of Sassanian silverwork and of the cliff reliefs at Taki Bostan. The freedom of the design suggests that the material was woven in Persia a little after the Sassanian period.

23.   Pheasant. Fragment.

24. Cock. Silk twill. Sassanian, 6th–7th century. Museo Sacro, Vatican.

fabrics and clothing in many of the graves at Antinoë. There were typical Sassanian silks decorated with winged horses and mountain goats similar to those on the cliff relief at Taki-Bostan carved in the reign of Khosru II (591–628), and quantities of borders and trimmings (some in silk, some in linen) with palmettes, horses, griffons and human heads. Their strong colours distinguished them from both earlier and later textiles.

Some of the silks in church treasures have similar designs, for example the silk twill at Sens with its pattern of lozenges containing alternate crosses and youthful head-and-shoulders portraits decorated with fluttering ribbons. Or the wonderful fragment in Aachen (plate 22) which shows a pair of peacocks, each holding a twig with three leaves in its beak. To what extent fabrics like this were also produced in Antinoë is still a matter for debate. It would appear that the large woollen fabric with horses and lions in the Dumbarton Oaks Collection is of an earlier date, since the borders with riders and lions are still in the Egyptian style. Yet even here, as in most of the other materials in this group, the animals stand on pedestals of various sorts.

The fascinating cloth from Lyons (plate 26) which shows a Sassanian king in battle, is definitely of Egyptian origin. It may have been part of a pair of breeches. Copying is even more apparent in another fabric from Antinoë at Lyons: the large woollen cloth with winged horses in circular surrounds, the discs of which are a favourite Sassanian device (plate

27). But we do not know whether the inhabitants of Antinoë were aware of the significance of the winged horse, which for the Persians represented the transfiguration of the god Verethragna, and also, like the ram, kingly power. The cockerel in the decorative roundel in the Bérard Collection in Paris (plate 29), however, is only slightly reminiscent of Sassanian originals.

Since very few pieces have survived, it is difficult to say what model the later Coptic fabrics followed, or to what extent they were original productions. And since argument still rages as to whether the silks were woven in Persia, Alexandria, Syria or Byzantium, it would be wise to ignore the whole question. In my opinion, the 6th- to 8th-century silk fabrics which have caused the most stir came from Syria; we shall return to them later.

Often the style is developed even further, particularly in places like Akhmim. Looking at the lovely woven portrait from Akhmim now in the Bérard Collection (plate 20), it is impossible to avoid being reminded of late painted mummy portraits, in spite of the fact that the material is 5th-century. The Detroit panel with the portrait of a man (plate 31) can hardly have been much later, but it represents a considerable development in style: the treatment is completely linear and the colours are no longer used realistically, though the man is still shown in semi-profile as in a double portrait in Berlin and in the Bawait frescoes.

The wonderful double portrait of Aurelius Colluthus and his wife, woven in Antinoë around

454–456, is already sufficiently stylised to show the figures full face. Perhaps the most important Egyptian woollen fabric is the large wall-hanging in the Dumbarton Oaks Collection (plate 32). An allegory, still completely in the classical spirit, it shows a seated woman with a nimbus round her head and above her the inscription *Hestia polyolbos*, 'the happy house'. Around her are six putti presenting her with the gifts of riches, happiness, good repute, generosity, virtue and progress. The composition is so superb that it brings to mind the Theodora mosaic in Ravenna, and the technique is so outstanding that it makes one wonder whether it was not the work of a Byzantine.

A whole series of textiles, showing two horsemen on a red ground riding away from or towards each other, ready for battle with sword and bow in hand, are probably modelled on Syrian originals such as the horsemen fabrics in Maastricht or London. In the roundel in Washington, the rider with the sword being crowned by two genii has been identified as Alexander. Here the 5th- or 6th-century artist was modelling his work on earlier sources like the Aachen pulpit or the bone reliefs in Baltimore and the Benaki Museum in Athens. In one fabric in the Cooper Union Museum in New York the rider is by himself. The closely related and well-preserved panel in Washington (plate 34) shows two horsemen fighting, as does another, very similar piece in the Cooper Union Museum (plate 33). A square purple panel with a rider design in London (plate 42) shows how in later years, certainly under Arab rule, this

25. Patterned material of silk twill. Iranian (?), 6th–7th century. Aachen Cathedral treasure.

26. Battle featuring a Sassanian king. Fragment. Wool.
Egyptian, 5th–6th century. Musée Historique des Tissus,
Lyons.

25.   Patterned material of silk twill. Height 67 cm. Iranian (?), 6th–7th century. Aachen Cathedral treasure. Patterned fruit baskets with handles forming a medallion-like design. The strong luminous colours and the stylised plant motif indicate a Near Eastern origin, although no instance of similar fruit baskets has yet been found in Sassanian art.

26.   Battle scene featuring a Sassanian king. Fragment of a pair of trousers; wool. Egyptian, from Antinoë; 5th–6th century. Musée Historique des Tissus, Lyons. Border of lozenges on a red ground. There is a matching fragment in the Louvre in Paris. The costume worn by the man on the throne indicates that he is a Sassanian king. Above him battle rages between his archers and black warriors, perhaps Ethiopians. Most likely a good copy (made in Antinoë) of a Sassanian fabric; but definitely not an import.

27.   Winged horses. Fragment, probably of a curtain; wool. Egyptian, from Antinoë; 5th–6th century. Musée Historique des Tissus, Lyons. The medallions have a red ground, and the direction in which the horses face alternates with each horizontal row. The treatment of the horses and the disc motif of the surrounds indicate that this fabric was probably copied from a Sassanian original. Sassanian silks of this type were found in Antinoë; some of them are now in Lyons and Berlin. This is a copy of the same kind as the battle scene in Lyons.

28.   Curtain with a design of horses and lions. Woollen fragment. Egyptian, from Antinoë; 5th century. Collection Dumbarton Oaks, Washington. Successive rows of flower-shaped capitals surmounted by the protomes of lions or horses, in pairs, facing in opposite directions. On the right, a border of lions and men on horseback in circular surrounds; this is typically Coptic while the horses and lions in the main part of the material are copied from a Sassanian silk, but of an earlier period than the winged horse or the battle scene fabrics in Lyons. Several specimens of this type of fabric were found in Antinoë; the bulk of them are now in Lyons, Paris and Berlin.

27. Winged horses. Fragment, probably of a curtain.

motif became so completely stylised as to be little more than an ornamental device.

The austere decoration of Sassanian and Syrian textiles also influenced the more ornamental fabrics. This includes the use of putti of the Christian type, as in the roundel in Berlin (plate 36). The central section of the border contains a floral motif reminiscent of Syrian silks and the centre-piece has a red ground with putti symmetrically arranged around a palmette. The development of ornamentation employing plant motifs exactly paralleled that of figural design. The lozenge and palmette pattern, for instance, originated from the type of heart-shaped leaf one can see in the Berlin roundel.

Equestrian designs and putti are, of course, unlikely to have had any connection with Christianity. But, on the other hand, in late Coptic times there were many textiles—panels, rectangular pieces of border and clavi—with scenes from the Old and New Testaments as well as portraits of saints. Many of them are so damaged that it is difficult to see what they are meant to represent, and it is not possible to say with any certainty whether or not the weavers were imitating Syrian silks or miniatures.

The favourite Old Testament subject was the story of Joseph; he was greatly revered in Egypt, especially in Alexandria. One of the most beautiful textiles with this theme came from Akhmim and is now in the Trier Museum (plate 39). It is similar to related panels in London, Berlin, Leningrad, Athens and Tarrasa as well as the sleeve-bands in Vienna. The centre-piece

28. Curtain with horses and lions. Woollen fragment. Egyptian, 5th century. Collection Dumbarton Oaks, Washington.

of the Trier fabric clearly shows Joseph's dream, while in the band round it, on a red ground, are scenes from his life: the young Joseph is sent to his brothers; his arrival and the scene at the stream; he is sold to the Ishmaelites; he departs.

The border consists of a pattern of palmettes; the panel in Leningrad may come from the same tunic. The Vienna panel, however, is so stylised that it is difficult to see who the figures are meant to represent, and the same applies to the *clavi*. Saints were a favourite subject on them; on the shoulder bands from Akhmim in Berlin (plate 41) the figures are still relatively easy to identify, but in other cases, such as the linen-based *clavi* in Trier (plate 40), also from Akhmim, with their three upright figures and their rosettes and fantastic animals above and below, the human figure has become almost purely ornamental. Specimens like this show a strong Islamic influence. Coptic weavers continued their work even in Tiraz, the workshop of the Islamic court, and they were still in evidence in Tinnis in the 12th century. It is possible that these somewhat coarse and gaudy cloths were bought mainly by the Coptic populace. Indeed, the Copts (that is, Christian Egyptians) were favourably looked upon up to the end of the 10th century, under the Tulunids (868–905) and the first Fatimids.

The later purple fabrics, in which the old Hellenistic motifs can still be recognised, became equally stylised, and the human figure was treated almost as a geometrical shape. Two fabrics from Berlin illustrate this: one a neckband with three orantes in the centre and one on each side (plate 43), the other a *clavus* (plate 44) in which the human figure is hardly recognisable.

In certain cases two-coloured silks, some of which bore the name of Zacharias or Joseph, were even given Arabic inscriptions. (Most of these were found in Akhmim.) The patterns included horsemen, as in the well-preserved London specimen (plate 45), saints, busts and palmette decoration, all to a great extent derived from Sassanian silks. The later pieces had been adapted to the Coptic style, with the result that the figures became rigid, as can be seen by comparing the man fighting a lion from the *clavi* (in Krefeld) made in the Zacharias workshops with the elegant design from the tomb of St Ambrosius in Milan.

While Coptic art in Egypt became more and more sterile and Coptic textiles fell increasingly under Islamic influence, the Byzantine Empire and Syria (including Antioch) now began their great period of development. Once again finds provide no definite proof of place of manufacture, and so it is necessary to rely on stylistic comparisons and, above all, written sources. The papal gifts recorded in the *Liber Pontificalis* and, for Byzantium itself, the imperial edicts, the prefects' book of the 10th century, and information in the work of Constantine VII Porphyrogenitus, provide a good point of departure. There are also church inventories, like that of Sens. All this information combined gives some idea of the various manufacturers and their different styles.

29. Cock. Fragment, originally a tondo. Wool on linen.
Egyptian, 5th century. Collection Bérard, Paris.

30. Curtain with two portraits. Wool on linen. Egyptian, 454–456. Musées d'Art et d'Histoire, Brussels.

29.   Cock. Fragment, originally a tondo. Wool on linen. Egyptian, from Akhmim; 5th century. Collection Bérard, Paris. The cock faces right and is set in a surround decorated with palmettes. One can still see traces of Sassanian influence. In the opinion of the owner of this fabric, the cock could be a Christian symbol: *'post tenebras lux'* (Jeremiah 31, 35).

30.   Curtain with two portraits; badly damaged. Wool on linen. Egyptian, from the tomb of Aurelius Colluthus in Antinoë. Papyri found with it date it somewhere between 454 and 456. Musées d'Art et d'Histoire, Brussels. The upper part contains a double portrait, probably of Aurelius Colluthus and his wife Tisoia; the lower, a pattern of lozenges containing vine leaves in between two pillars. The stylisation of the portraits is indicative of the transition to the Coptic style then taking place.

31.   Portrait of a man. Fragment of wool and linen on linen. Egyptian, 5th century. Institute of Arts, Detroit. A head-and-shoulders portrait of a man in an oval surround; he has a nimbus and is looking to the right. The effect is of a rather belated version of a mummy portrait, but the design is so stylised as to be almost abstract.

32.   Hestia polyolbos; slightly damaged. Height 1·13 m. Wool on linen. Egyptian, 4th–5th century. Collection Dumbarton Oaks, Washington. Round the goddess of the domestic hearth are six putti bearing gifts and two allegorical figures, the one on the right representing light, the one on the left a poet. One of the most beautiful Egyptian woollen fabrics to have survived. Still completely in the spirit of classical humanism—witness the putti offering the gifts of Peace, Progress, Wealth and Virtue—yet almost Coptic in its two-dimensional quality.

32. Goddess of the domestic hearth. Wool on linen. Egyptian, 4th–5th century. Collection Dumbarton Oaks, Washington.

In due course, one hopes, finds will be made like those at Palmyra or Antinoë, and the study of reliquary cloths from various church treasures will increase the amount of available evidence. Important fabrics have certainly been discovered in recent years —at Rheims, St Calais, Le Monastier and Trier, for instance—though it is doubtful whether there will ever be another stroke of luck like the discovery of the collection of reliquaries in the Sancta Sanctorum in Rome. But now that experts of all nations have joined forces to form CIETA ('Centre international d'Etude des Textiles anciens') in Lyons, it is to be hoped that between them they will make more efficient use of existing information.

The *Liber Pontificalis*, which has been published by Duchesne, besides giving descriptions of the various fabrics, also provides important clues as to their provenance. The accounts go up to Benedict XIII (855–858), and it is sad to realise what a wealth of early textiles there were in Rome alone, and that all of them have vanished. In the *Liber Pontificalis*, under Leo IV and Lothair, we read: '*Historia aquilarum, storia de elefantos, istoria pavonum portantium de super homines et aliam historiam aquilarum rotarumque et arium cum arboribus pendentem in arcum triumphalem habentem in medio Adnunciatio et nativitatem D. n. J. C., Cristus, Maria, 12 Apostoli, Maria cum Pietro et Paule et donatore.*' Pope Paschal I (817–824) wore '*vestem chrisoclavam ex auro gemmisque cum facibus accensionis, storia Danielis, storia sanctorum Joachim et Annae.*' One can just see them! Curtains and wall-hangings are also described: '*vela per arcos presbiterii, vela paschales "in diebus festis", in natale Apostolorum, per cotidianis diebus, in circuitu altaris, in ingressu presbiterii, per arcos presbiterii*.' And the materials are given too: '*ex auro, cum auro, aurotextile, vestem auro textam, candidis per totum margaritis fulgentem*', that is, set with precious stones—which is corroborated by the information from Monte Cassino.

New Testament scenes, like Jesus in the Temple and the Crucifixion, are very common: '*Storia Passionis, storia Crucifixi*.' Again with reference to Paschal I: '*Nativitatem seu Assumptionem eiusdem in emeratae Virginis*', that is, an Ascension like the one at Sens. We see Leo III and St Peter '*vestem crysoclabam habentem historiam letaniae maioris*.' But most important of all are the provenances: '*vestem siricam, de chrisoclabo cum orbiculis et rotas siricas*.' Under Leo III the following material was ordered for S. Apollinare in Ravenna: '*fecit vestem siricam rosatam albam, habentem in medio crucem de chrisoclabo cum orbiculis et rosas siricas habentes storia Adnuntiatione seu natale D. n. J.C. atque Passionem et Resurrectionem, nec non et in caelis Ascensionem atque Pentecostem*.'

It is interesting to note that in places where a considerable amount of cloth was required, for curtains (*vela*) between pillars, before a triumphal arch, or in front of an entrance, cheaper, possibly Alexandrian, silks were bought. For really important places, however, in the ciborium or in the presbytery, round the bishop's throne, heavy Syrian costume fabrics were preferred. The *Liber Pontificalis* lists: silk from

Syria ('*de Tyreo*' or '*diaspro de Antiochis*'), Byzantium ('*de blati bizantea*'), Alexandria ('*panum alexandrinum*') and later from Cyprus ('*de opere cyprensi*') and Asia ('*de panno tartarico*'). It is not until around 800 that we read of the first cloth of Italian manufacture ('*una fabbrica napoletana*'). Churches also needed precious stuffs to cover altars, chalices and patens and the tombs of saints ('*pallia, oppure mafortes*'). The 'Charta Cornutiana' of 471, which refers to a small church near Tivoli, shows how well even small churches were endowed with valuable textiles. Maximian, Bishop of Ravenna (546–556), was very generous: according to the *Liber Pontificalis* he donated a curtain decorated with the story of Christ and his own portrait.

It did not take the Northern churches long to more or less catch up with their Italian counterparts. At the beginning of the 9th century there were more than 80 pallia and curtains at St Riquier, 20 at St Wandrille, 40 at Flavigny, 35 at Marchiennes and 20 at Clermont. Though they were used to decorate altars and the tombs of saints, they were primarily intended for the walls, arcades and doors. The most valuable were used as wall-hangings only on feast days. Gregory of Tours once had a basilica decorated with expensive snow-white pallia embroidered with purple silk and in the 7th century, according to the *Gesta Dagobert*, the whole nave of St Denis in Paris was hung with gold-embroidered fabrics set with pearls. Gregory of Tours also relates that when, under Sigisbert, St Denis was on fire, a soldier stole some silk pallia from the saint's grave, and Einhard records that, 'according

33. Decorative roundel with two horsemen. Wool on linen. Egyptian, 6th century. Cooper Union Museum, New York.

34. Decorative roundel with two horsemen. Wool on linen.
Egyptian, 6th century. Textile Museum, Washington.

33.   Decorative roundel with two horsemen. Wool on linen. Egyptian, 6th century. Cooper Union Museum, New York. Two horsemen, one on either side of the Tree of Life, ride towards each other with drawn swords. In the tree are two confronting lions. This fabric closely resembles the horseman fabric in Washington (plate 34), and like it is copied from a Syrian silk.

34.   Decorative roundel with two horsemen. Wool on linen. Egyptian, 6th century. Textile Museum, Washington. A hunting scene: the rider on the left brandishes a sword, the other is driving his spear into a lion. Like the material shown in plate 33 it is modelled on a Syrian silk. In the same collection is a similar

35

fabric with riders who have been identified as emperors because the material has the name Alexander inscribed on it. Comparisons might also be made with the triumphant emperors on an ivory diptych in Paris or with the horseman on the fabric in Aachen.

35.   Material with a medallion pattern. Wool on linen. Egyptian, 6th–7th century. Städtisches Museum, Trier. Two small roundels on either side of a larger one with a badly repaired design showing Samson. Each of the smaller roundels contains two horsemen. The material is interesting because it shows the changeover to the Coptic style much more clearly than the horsemen fabrics in New York and Washington.

to a Frankish custom', the shrine of St Marcellinus and St Peter was covered with silks and linen, and that above it there was a baldachin of precious cloth. The outer casing of St Paulinus' sarcophagus in Trier was lined inside and out with silk, as was that of St Modoaldus in the church of St Paulinus, also in Trier.

The majority of these textiles were certainly imported. In 461 Sidonius Apollinaris mentions a beautiful Sassanian-style material from Meliboea in Thessaly. After the Mohammedan conquest most of the fabrics that crossed the Danube and the Rhine finally found their way to France. Like almost all the early fabrics still in existence they came from the Near East: the horseman material in Lyons and the eagle fabric in Auxerre are Byzantine, King Robert's chasuble in Toulouse is Hispano-Moorish, St Cecilia's shroud in Albi is Islamic.

Descriptions cannot really give any idea of the wealth of precious fabrics in Byzantium. Hagia Sophia and the other large churches, as well as the various palaces, must have been filled with silks and wall-hangings donated by the emperors, not to mention the magnificent imperial robes and those of the high officials. The mosaics in San Vitale, Ravenna, show magnificent examples of the latter. Justinian is on one side of the presbytery and Theodora on the other, in the middle of a circle of court officials wearing their purple robes. The Empress's costume, with its elaborately embroidered Adoration of the Magi on the hem, is superb. The clothes her attendants wear are rich and colourful too, but the patterns are simpler, consisting of random decorative motifs like those on the fragments in the Sancta Sanctorum or in the imperial mosaics in Hagia Sophia in Constantinople. The same delightful garments can also be seen in miniatures—those in the Paris manuscripts, for instance—of emperors like Nicephorus Botaniates (1078–1081) or, in a somewhat later style, of the Grand Admiral Apokandos (c. 1342). The ivory reliefs with portraits of the consuls between Areobindus (506) and Justinus (541) are also important as far as dating fabric designs of this kind is concerned. Rich ceremonial garments, cloaks in particular, are generally decorated with simple, small ornamental motifs like rosettes, squares or lozenges. The Empress's dalmatic on the ivory diptych in Florence is more elaborate with its portrait of the young Leo Minor (c. 500). Such designs may well have been embroidered.

The trade in these luxury items was carefully controlled in the capital. The shops that sold cloth were next to the hippodrome near the baths of Zeuxippos. Here, according to Cedrenus, one could buy silk (*sericae*) or cloth of gold (*chrysobasta*). Many specialists worked in the palace workshops. There was one shop that produced nothing but gold bands (*clavi aurei*). It was in these workshops that purple was made into dye and the raw silk was prepared, so they contained dyers, weavers and artists. All this was controlled by the prefect, who saw to it that the finished cloth was stamped with the appropriate seal. And since imported fabrics were sold through another state-controlled network, there was an imperial monopoly in silk. The palace itself employed a large staff of tailors to make and repair clothes for the imperial household. Justinian's introduction of silkworms into Constantinople brought about an immediate and significant increase in silk production. After Heraclius's victory over Khosru II (638), a vast amount of raw silk, clothes, carpets and embroidery was brought back to Byzantium, and as a result the palace was furnished with wonderful carpets. Ready-made clothes were also imported from Syria, where Tyre and Berytus possessed the most thriving work-shops. Textiles also came from Sidon. Syrian cloth was sold in Jerusalem, and one could buy Egyptian clothes in the forum in Constantinople. A further batch of valuable textiles, such as carpets containing gold thread, reached the capital after Belisarius's victory over the Vandals. As a result, Constantinople had become a great centre of the textile industry.

Purple, of which there were three separate types, remained an imperial monopoly for even longer than other stuffs. After the iconoclast controversy there was no compulsion to join a guild, but the guilds nonetheless re-established themselves under Leo VI (911–912). In the 10th century a complete silk industry arose, organised in five guilds: those who dealt in raw silk (*Metaxoprates*); those who made it into thread (*Katartarii*); the weavers (*Serikarii*); those who sold silk clothing (*Bestioprates*); and those who dealt in Syrian silk (*Prandioprates*). Foreigners could only buy the cheaper fabrics, and even then only for their

36. Roundel with putti. Wool on linen. Egyptian, 5th–6th century. Staatliche Museen, Berlin.

37. Roundel of the Adoration of the Magi. Wool on linen. Egyptian, 5th–6th century. Collection Bérard, Paris.

38. Material with figural design. Egyptian. Musée du Louvre, Paris.

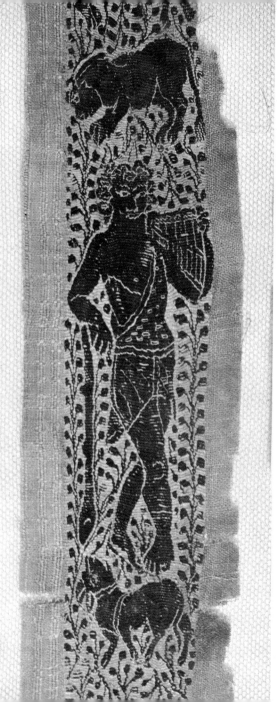

36.   Roundel with putti. Wool on linen. Egyptian, 5th–6th century. Staatliche Museen, Berlin. Large central field in a triple surround. Putti with fishing rods are shown above and to each side of a palmette; two of them have caught dolphins. The design is still influenced by the Nile variant of the Hellenistic style.

37.   Roundel of the Adoration of the Magi. Wool on linen. The upper part is damaged. Egyptian, from Akhmim; 5th–6th century. Collection Bérard, Paris. Mary, with the infant Jesus in her lap, sits on the left. Probably a copy of a Syrian silk, but the style has been changed. There are textiles with similar subjects in Berlin and London.

38.   Material with figural design. Egyptian. Louvre, Paris. The modelling on the figure gives it a certain plastic quality, and the animals and other details of the design suggest that it represents a shepherd.

39.   Roundel of Joseph's dream. Wool on linen. Part of the border has been torn away. Egyptian, from Akhmim; 6th century. Städtisches Museum, Trier. The central medallion shows Joseph's dream. Round it are scenes from his life: he is sent to his brothers as a child; his arrival and the scene at the stream; he is sold to the Ishmaelites; his departure. There are many similar fabrics, for instance in Berlin, London, Leningrad, Athens and Tarasa. This particular one provides a very good example of how Syrian silk designs were adapted by the Copts.

39. Roundel of Joseph's dream.

own use. Travellers' baggage was carefully searched, and Liutprand, Bishop of Cremona (950–972), was once arrested for smuggling. Favoured states were granted special concessions, Kievan Russia being the most privileged in this respect. In fact in 907, after Oleg of Kiev's campaign, Russia no longer had to pay any duty at all. The cloth trade with the German Empire, which was considered illegal, was made more difficult, and so, incidentally, was trade with Bulgaria.

In spite of this there is an abundance of these precious fabrics throughout the West. Italian merchants in Amalfi and Venice played an important part in importing them, the trade being concentrated in Pavia. Many of these 'Byzantine' fabrics may equally well have been woven in Greece. Rabbi Benjamin of Tudela (1160–1173) states that in Thebes in the Peloponnese about 2,000 Jews were employed in the manufacture of silk and purple fabrics. Some of the cloth was sent to Byzantium where, according to Benjamin, 2,500 Jews worked in Pera.

In view of the great demand for these precious stuffs, similar workshops were set up outside Greece. Isidore of Seville records that cloth was made there. Such silk fabrics as the one with hippocampi and elephants in Berlin or the one with a lion design in Amsterdam may have been copied in Spain from Byzantine originals. In Italy fabric designs evidently influenced relief carving (in Campania, for instance— particularly the reliefs at Sorrento), so the existence of decorative animal reliefs in several Spanish churches can be taken to prove that there were large numbers of such fabrics in Spain under the Visigoths.

Garments made of Byzantine cloth became status symbols—in other countries, as in Byzantium itself. Consequently, certain feudatories outside the capital obtained permission to farm silk for their private use. They kept what cloth they required, and sold the surplus to the Bestioprates.

Relatively few of the fabrics woven in the Middle Ages (that is, after the reign of Justinian I) have survived compared with the numbers that, according to written sources, once existed. It was greatly to Otto von Falke's credit that, as early as 1913, he was fairly successful in classifying the surviving specimens according to date and provenance. New discoveries have naturally necessitated a few changes. Nowadays, for example, the heavy silk compound twills with their designs on a red ground (the Annunciation and the Adoration in the Vatican, the Samsons in London and in the Dumbarton Oaks Collection, the Säckingen Amazons and the quadriga in Brussels) are no longer attributed to Alexandria. It is more likely that light silks, for example the one with horsemen in Düsseldorf or the Zacharias silks, were produced there. To judge by their style and lavishness, the heavier cloths probably came from one of the Syrian centres. Some were also of more recent manufacture than von Falke thought, since we know a few were made specifically for reliquaries which themselves originated only in the 9th century. Also suggestive of a Syrian origin is the still evident relationship with Hellenistic originals, whereas Byzantine work is more stylised and predominantly influenced by Persia. My personal opinion is that the quadriga fabric in Aachen and the horsemen in combat in Cologne, Prague, Milan and St Calais also fall into this category.

Two large silk panels with a design of a Sassanian king hunting, which were in Berlin until they were lost after the war, show how strongly the styles favoured by the Byzantine court were influenced by Persian art. Until recently they were thought to be Sassanian and, because they showed a Sassanian king stabbing a lion and, even more indicative, wearing a very unusual crown, they were assumed to represent Yezdegerd III. One of these panels came from St Ursula's in Cologne, the other from Trier. In the latter the king holds a young lion in one hand and a falcon in the other; perhaps, because of the young lion, it should be taken as representing king Bahram Gor. The crown, the costume and the winged horse all indicate a Sassanian origin, and there are stylistic similarities with Persian silver, for example with one of the plates in the British Museum. But, as Smirnov has already pointed out, there are several slight inexactitudes in the clothing which indicate that the panel is in fact one of the best copies of Sassanian fabrics in existence. Another, later instance of Byzantine copying can be seen in the late-11th-century enamel plaques on the Pala d'Oro in Venice, which again show a Sassanian emperor hunting with a falcon.

Not many Near Eastern fabrics bearing Christian motifs seem to have survived from the centuries after the close of antiquity. But there are some with patterns similar to those on garments in consular diptychs which may possibly date from the time of the iconoclast controversy. Especially important is a silk twill from the Madelbert shrine in Liège, which has a lozenge pattern containing the Greek monogram HPAKLIOY. This monogram is similar to one appearing on certain silver plates, and has been connected with Heraclius, which also agrees with the stylistic evidence. Other lozenge-patterned fabrics of this kind—the very closely related type with palmettes and cocks in Berlin, Lyons and elsewhere, and similar ones in Marburg an der Lahn—also come into this category. The high degree of stylisation of these two-coloured fragments points to Constantinople as their place of origin.

Somewhat later in date are the silks von Falke attributed to Alexandria. They are closely related to each other in design, ornamentation and colour. The floral surrounds in particular are very similar and indicate the same Hellenistic connections we noted when dealing with Egyptian cloths. Among the earliest, in my opinion, is the much-admired silk with the design of a man fighting a lion (plate 48). The man, dressed in a short tunic and a chlamys, is forcing the lion's jaws apart. Some authorities think the figure represents Daniel, because the existence of such a cloth was recorded in Rome at the time of Gregory IV (827–844): '*de Tyrio, habentem historiam*

41

40. Decorative bands. Wool and linen on linen. Egyptian, 7th–8th century. Städtisches Museum, Trier.

41. Decorative band. Wool on linen. Egyptian, 7th–8th century. Staatliche Museen, Berlin.

40.   Decorative bands. Wool and linen on linen. Egyptian, from Akhmim; 7th–8th century. Städtisches Museum, Trier. The central section of each band shows three standing female figures. Above and below them are fantastic animals. There are similar motifs showing the same stylistic changes on a *clavus* in Berlin and on a roundel *(orbiculus) in Brussels*. These bands may even date from the Islamic period.

41.   Decorative band. Wool on linen. Egyptian, from Akhmim; 7th–8th century. Staatliche Museen, Berlin. The central strip is divided into red and blue rectangles. In each of the rectangles with a red ground stands the figure of a saint, looking to his right. There are similar bands with the same single figures in Turin, Munich, and elsewhere. The figures here are already little more than abstract decorations.

42.   Rectangular panel with a horseman. Wool on linen. Egyptian, from Akhmim; 6th–7th century. Victoria and Albert Museum, London. Decorative panel from a brown woollen tunic. The rider holds a garland in his right hand. The border is decorated with stylised acanthus leaves. Last phase of the so-called 'purple stuffs'. The original Hellenistic patterns are now scarcely recognisable.

43.   Panel with a pattern of figures. Wool on linen. Egyptian, 6th–8th century. Staatliche Museen, Berlin. Only the *clavi* and the front part of the tunic have survived. Praying figures provide the decoration. The three in a row at the top stand in separate bays of an arcade of spiral pillars; they represent a complete stylistic adaptation. There is a tunic in this style, and in good condition, at Trier.

42. Rectangular panel with a horseman.

43. Panel with a pattern of figures. Wool on linen. Egyptian, 6th–8th century. Staatliche Museen, Berlin.

Danielis.' The design on the famous Cyprian silver plate (now in Nicosia) also springs to mind in this context. But this identification has now apparently been rejected in favour of the alternative, Samson. No other early silk found its way into so many church treasures: there are fragments in Coire, Dumbarton Oaks, Berlin, Düsseldorf, Nuremberg, Ottobeuren, Florence, Trent, Lyons, London, Maastricht and Vienna.

The design also has points of correspondence with the exquisite Aachen fragment of a man fighting a lion and the Säckingen Amazon cloth in Berlin and Freiburg im Breisgau. Whereas similar designs are set in circular surrounds, the Samson fabric, despite the fact that its design is repetitive, has only a simple border. A date as late as the end of the 8th century is given to it because the fragment in Ottobeuren was used to wrap the relics of St Alexander when they were removed from Rome during the reign of Charlemagne. This date is supported by stylistic evidence provided by similar silks. Little remains of the fragment in the Kofler-Truniger Collection in Lucerne (plate 50), but its design—an archer shooting at a lion—is very close to that of the Samson cloth, and the archer's attitude is very reminiscent of that of the two bare-breasted Amazons with their chitons and chlamys in the Säckingen material in Berlin and Freiburg. Here too, a circular floral surround is used. Two cloths of Egyptian origin, one in the Victoria and Albert Museum in London and the other in Maastricht, provide further close parallels, for both contain a naturalistic representation of a man fighting a lion with a bow and arrow.

The quadriga fabric from Münsterbilsen (plate 49) now in Brussels is clearly based on a much earlier original. The heart-shaped flowers of the circular surround and the subject it contains give ample proof of the connection with the horseman fabrics described earlier. One suggestion put forward is that the man driving the quadriga is a charioteer in the hippodrome. But the design could equally well represent Alexander's entry into heaven.

To what extent the 'Dioscuri' material in Maastricht can be said to belong to the horseman group is difficult to say. The design and the ornamentation are harsher and the duplication of the standing figure, the god receiving a sacrifice, shows how long a heathen motif could survive.

Our classification now brings us to the two most famous silks of all (plates 51 and 52), which are fragments of the same material, a compound twill in five colours. Their subjects are the Annunciation and the Nativity; they originally came from the church treasure of the Capella Sancta Sanctorum but are now in the Museo Sacro of the Vatican Library. In each piece the Madonna's robe is dyed with real purple. The fragments are identical in size and style of decoration, although Pfister identified two different reds in them. But particularly striking is the similarity of their ornamental motifs of heart-shaped leaves and large palmettes between the circular surrounds.

In the Annunciation Mary sits on a throne set with precious stones, and the archangel, dressed in a white tunic with brown stripes, approaches her from the right with his right hand held up as if addressing her. In the Nativity, Mary, again seated, has a brown nimbus and wears a purple mantle. Her feet, in red shoes, rest on a footstool. Joseph is opposite her.

The design, colour and technique correspond to those of the five-coloured horsemen fabrics, and the date of origin cannot be much different from that of the Samson material—which means it was probably woven towards the end of the 8th century and, like the materials mentioned above, in a Christian part of the Near East, perhaps Syria. We also know from the *Liber Pontificalis* that Leo III (795–816) made a gift of a material *'rota sirica habentes storias Adnuntiatione seu Natale Domini Nostri Jesu Cristi'*. This reinforces the theory of a Syrian origin, even if the palmettes are still almost Sassanian and are clearly related to Byzantine work. But if the date of origin is correct, it is surprising that a fabric with a figurative subject should have been woven during the iconoclast controversy.

The iconography of the Nativity scene can be linked with such Syrian work as the scene on the lid of a wooden reliquary from Palestine (now in the Sancta Sanctorum) or on the ampulla in Monza. In view of this, Falke and Langman's theory that it was made in Alexandria in the first half of the 6th century should be rejected.

Close links such as those between Syria and the

44. *Clavus* with male figures. Wool on linen. Fragment Egyptian, 6th–8th century. Staatliche Museen, Berlin.

45. Part of a decorative sleeveband with two horsemen.
Silk. Egyptian, 6th–8th century. Victoria and Albert Museum,
London.

44. *Clavus* with male figures. Wool on linen. Fragment. Egyptian, 6th–8th century. Staatliche Museen, Berlin. The central band is divided into rectangles which are decorated with a mass of small animals, with male figures or with horsemen. In its treatment of the human figure almost as an abstract this material shows affinities with Islamic art.

45. Part of a decorative sleeveband with two horsemen. Silk. Egyptian, from Akhmim; 6th–8th century. Victoria and Albert Museum, London. Each of the horsemen is being attacked by a small male figure with a spear. Above the figures is the inscription 'Zachariou'. The ornamentation of the upper section reveals Sassanian influence. There are further examples of these silks, mostly from Akhmim, in Berlin, London and elsewhere.

46. Part of a medallion with two horsemen. Silk. 8th century. Sant'Ambrogio, Milan. Used to cover the inner faces of the doors of the gold altar (835) of Sant'Ambrogio. The riders hunt with bows and arrows, and their chlamys flutter behind them. Below each horse are a lion and a wild ass struck through with the same arrow. The rider has been identified with the Sassanian King Bahram V Gor (420–438), who was given the cognomen Gor (wild ass) as a result of this legendary feat. There are other examples of this type of cloth, based on a Sassanian original, in Prague, in the diocesan museum in Cologne (the cloth used to be in the Church of St Cunibert) and in St Calais. It is also clearly connected with the horsemen fabric in Maastricht (plate 47).

47. Medallion with two horsemen. Silk. Syrian (?), 7th century. Church treasure of St Servatius, Maastricht. Only one half of the medallion has survived. The horsemen hunt with bows. This fabric is more in the Hellenistic idiom than those in Prague or Milan (plate 46). The heart-shaped flower decoration of the surrounds points to Syria as its place of origin. It is also worth comparing it with the horseman motif in plate 45 and with the huntsman on foot in plate 50.

46.   Part of a medallion with two horsemen.

47. Medallion with two horsemen. Silk. Syrian (?), 7th century. Church treasure of St Servatius, Maastricht.

Persian Empire, already well in evidence by 361, when Shapur II brought silk weavers from Mesopotamia and Syria to Persia, were beginning to be established with countries to the north because Byzantium saw itself increasingly threatened by the Persian monopoly. So, after capturing Khosru II's base (624), Heraclius brought skilled silk weavers with him to Byzantium, where they continued to work in their native tradition. We have already seen how much Egypt, and Antinoë in particular, was influenced by Persian textiles up to the time of the Mohammedan conquest. Space does not permit an exploration of the relationship between Sassanian weaving and that of the East, particularly Central Asia, China and Japan. The Sassanian silk with the boar's-head design found in Astana (Chinese Turkestan) and the textiles in Nara, which show the Mikado Shōmu (died 756) out hunting, indicate how close this relationship was.

The fact that the Persians had a virtual monopoly of the importation of raw silk into the Mediterranean area meant that they were in a position to export their own goods to the East. By carefully studying the cliff reliefs around Persepolis and Taki-Bostan, which depict one of the later emperors, Khosru II (590–628), Herzfeld was able to identify about 30 different textile patterns. Combined with a comparative study of Sassanian silver plate—there are superb specimens in Teheran, the Hermitage in Leningrad and various American museums—and other examples of applied art, such as the delightful

Khosru goblet in the Bibliothèque Nationale in Paris, this gives us a fairly good idea of the various types of Sassanian textiles. These fabrics were so perfectly designed and so beautifully made that in the early Middle Ages they became a model for the rest of the known world. Even the early silks from Antinoë, with their extravagant patterns and historical representations (for example the hunting scenes in Cologne and Trier), are of a quality which makes it comprehensible that for centuries architectural decorative sculpture as well as weaving sought inspiration in them.

The later fabrics can be roughly dated by comparing them with the one in which King Yezdegerd rides on a horned griffon: they must have been woven before the middle of the 8th century. A nine-coloured material from Antinoë (now in Lyons and Paris) also comes into this category. It shows a king, possibly Khosru I, fighting the Ethiopians, and is remarkable for the realism and vigour with which the combatants are depicted. It hardly matters whether the fabric is a good Coptic copy or an original work.

Materials with animal motifs are the most common of all surviving Sassanian textiles. The animals are generally shown singly in a surround decorated with a row of discs, though the cliff reliefs include several patterns without surrounds. Antinoë also produced some typical examples of these, namely cloths with winged horse and mountain goat motifs. They can be identified as Sassanian by comparing them with the cliff reliefs. One of the most important specimens of this type is the hippocampus material, one piece of which is in London (plate 21) and the other in Paris. The same motif occurs on silverwork and, most important, on the king's trousers in Taki-Bostan. But it is possible, as Herzfeld maintains, that this part of the relief was carved some hundred years before the time of Khosru II and is in a still older style modelled on an Assyrian or Babylonian original; it may even have been influenced by Greek hippocampi. The use of this motif on fabrics from Antinoë has already been remarked.

The two most beautiful specimens of all came from the treasure of the Sancta Sanctorum and are now in the Vatican. The earliest of the two has a bird like a duck (or a pheasant) on a greyish white ground (plate 23). The bird has a twig in its beak and a blue band round its neck. It too is reminiscent of the cliff reliefs and is closely related to the hippocampus material. The geese in the 8th- or 9th-century cloth in Aachen represent a later version of the same subject. A similar bird appears in a fresco in Kyzyl (Turfan), which shows how widespread this motif was.

The famous cock fabric (plate 24), however, is surer in its execution and represents a considerable advance. Its technical perfection—it has a weft of six, sometimes seven, threads—is one of the reasons why it is so precious. The design is in ten colours, with three different turquoises alone, and the threads on the back of the fabric have been left free. In style it is very similar to the pheasant/duck fabric and is therefore thought by almost all experts to be purely Sassanian; but in my opinion there are a number of reasons for believing it is related to early Islamic textiles.

Looking at these animal designs (and also some of the purely ornamental patterns), we have to ask the same question as we did about the two Berlin fabrics with the design of a Sassanian king hunting: are they Sassanian originals, or are they in fact Byzantine copies? Again, in spite of the fact that its Sassanian bell-shaped palmette appears to be somewhat degenerate in form, the strong colours and severity of the delightful material now in the Aachen Cathedral treasure (plate 25) make me believe that it is more likely to be of Persian than Byzantine origin. Still, this extremely elaborate material is a somewhat isolated case.

The large Byzantine hippocampus cloth, of which there are examples still in good condition in Brussels (plate 57) and in the Bargello in Florence, is a replica of a Sassanian original. The dragon with a peacock's tail is the same, but the colours (a dark purple and a blue-black ground) are different; in fact these colours were not used in Persian textiles at all. The combined evidence of a cushion from the tomb of St Remigius and a large piece of red silk (2·30 m. × 1·90 m.) which was only recently discovered in Rheims and is known to have come from the church of St Remi, provide an approximate date for the hippocampus material. The border of the cushion has a dedication from the 'famous' Bishop Hincmar, and the same Hincmar

48. Samson (David?) and the lion. Fragment. Silk twill.
Syrian (?), 7th–8th century. Victoria and Albert Museum,
London.

48. Samson (David?) and the lion. One of two fragments. Silk twill. Syrian (?), 7th century. Victoria and Albert Museum, London. This fabric is close in both style and technique to the heavy silks with red grounds like the Aachen lion-hunter fabric and the Amazon material from Säckingen. Earlier than the Maastricht horsemen (plate 47). It was apparently one of the most popular types of cloth, so numerous fragments have survived in church treasures. There are specimens in the Sancta Sanctorum in Rome, in Coire, Trento, Lyons, Paris, Florence, Düsseldorf, Nuremberg, Berlin, Maastricht, Vienna, Ottobeuren and the Dumbarton Oaks Collection, Washington.

49. Material with a pattern of quadrigas in medallions. Silk twill. Fragment; three and a half medallions (diameter 22 cm.) have survived. Reliquary cloth from the shrine of the abbess Landrada (c. 680–690) in Münsterbilsen. Syrian (?), 7th century. Musées d'Art et d'Histoire, Brussels. The charioteer is driving a racing chariot and two genii hover beside him, ready to hand him the victor's wreath. The motif is a common one.

49

50.　Medallion with huntsmen on foot. Silk twill. Fragment in two pieces. Syrian (?), 7th century. Collection Kofler-Truniger, Lucerne. The central design consists of two men, armed with bows and wearing short tunics, hunting a wild animal. The surround is decorated with heart-shaped flowers. One side is a mirror image of the other. The tunics are white with dark decorative panels like those on the silk fabrics in London and Maastricht (plates 45, 48). The fabric with horsemen in the church of St Ursula in Cologne and the Samson fabric reproduced in plate 48 also belong to this group.

51.　Nativity. Silk serge. Fragment. Syrian (?), 8th century. Museo Sacro, Vatican. Only one medallion has survived and the left part of this is missing. Cochineal may have been used for the red of the ground. It belongs to the identically styled fabric shown in plate 52, and like it came from the Sancta Sanctorum. Also very close in style to the Samson material (plate 48) and the Maastricht horsemen (plate 47). Its sheer weight differentiates it from Egyptian silks.

50. Medallion with huntsmen on foot. Silk twill. Fragment in two pieces. Syrian (?), 7th century. Collection Kofler-Truniger, Lucerne.

51. Nativity. Silk serge. Fragment. Syrian (?), 8th century.
Museo Sacro, Vatican.

had asked Alpheide, the sister of Charles the Bald, to embroider such a cushion for the saint's head when the church was consecrated in 852. The red cloth that covered the corpse had a similar pattern of hippo-campi in circular surrounds.

Even more stylised is the senmurv motif on a large piece of cloth closely related to the material just dis-cussed (plate 61). It too is in the Bargello in Florence. In this case the senmurv—the Sassanian royal device —is combined with both of the other favourite Sassanian animals: the winged horse and the elephant. The fabric is also typically Sassanian in its use of medallions with rows of discs as surrounds. The peculiarly harsh colouring can be explained by the fact that the material was not woven in Byzantium, as Falke maintained, but in a provincial workshop, possibly in Spain. Various fabrics connected with the Spanish peninsula, for example the lion material in Maastricht and the elephant material (now in Berlin) originally made for a Spanish church, appear to substantiate this point of view.

The Sassanian winged horse fabrics found in Antinoë show how exact the Byzantine copies are. The subject has of course lost its symbolic significance —the transfiguration of the god Verethragna—but the design itself has changed very little. The fluttering ribbons and the frontal presentation of the wings remain typical. A cushion in the Sancta Sanctorum on which the enamel crucifix of Pope Paschal I (817–824) was displayed is the best example of this type of fabric (plate 60); and, what is more, it can be dated.

The two winged horse materials in the Hanover Museum are already further away from the Persian style.

As it would take far too long to enumerate all the mythical beasts borrowed by Byzantine artists, I will mention only the lovely griffon fabrics; the best example is probably the Siviard sudarium in the Sens Cathedral treasure. The winged griffon stands by itself within a rather grandiose surround (65 cm. diameter; white on white and gold). The material was probably one of the very expensive ones made in the court workshops. Perhaps more primitive and possibly earlier (8th-century) is the stylised double-griffon design on such materials as the one in Leningrad, which came from a grave at Hassaonte in the Caucasus, or the specimen in the Church of St Martin's in Liège. One of the most beautiful animal designs of all is a griffon fragment which turned up not so long ago in Le Monastier (Haute Loire), where it formed part of the reliquary of St Theophrede (St Chaffre). Though the original on which it is based has not yet been found, it is a typical copy of a Persian design. The griffon is on a red ground, and holds a quadruped in its jaws. The striking use of colour, which also applies to the birds underneath it, is still very reminiscent of Near Eastern originals.

The Le Monastier griffon at once reminds the spectator of the design of an emperor fighting a lion on the large piece of material from Mozac (plate 55). (There is also a fragment in the Bargello.) This can be roughly dated since it is thought to be the reliquary cloth that Pippin the Short donated to the church in

761. It is a large panel of the type with yellow and white on a blue ground, in a surround about 60 cm. in diameter. The emperor, who is thrusting a spear at a lion, is shown in Persian costume on either side of the Tree of Life. The influence of the Persian original is still very apparent, even if not quite so obvious as in the case of the fabrics (in Berlin) from Trier and Cologne; but the more naturalistic presentation and the mistakes of detail in the depiction of court dress prove beyond doubt that it is of 8th-century Byzantine origin. Unfortunately only the emperor's head has survived from a similar fabric in Gandersheim.

The quadriga silk from the tomb of Charlemagne (died 814) is perhaps a little later. One half (plate 56) is still in Aachen, the other in the Cluny Museum in Paris. The design shows a circus scene in the lower part of which two boys are distributing gifts—a subject already familiar from consular diptychs. This material is more reminiscent of the 'Syrian' group of textiles. The decoration on the border is similar to that of the Säckingen Amazon material.

There is a peculiar mixture of styles in the silk with the lion-hunter design from the Sancta Sanctorum in the Vatican (plate 59). The strong colours (red, yellow, green, white and azure) with the undyed inner weft are almost the same as in Spanish materials. The design, however, with its costume decorated with red clavi and its ornamental surrounds, is more clearly Byzantine—of course with Sassanian influences—than the Mozac fabric in Lyons. It is also

52. Annunciation. Silk serge. Syrian (?), 8th century.
Museo Sacro, Vatican.

53. Reconstruction of the material reproduced in plate 54.

54. Lozenge pattern with leaves in the shape of a cross. Silk serge. Byzantine, 7th century. Musée Diocésan, Liège.

52.   Annunciation. Decorative band, of silk serge; double warp. From the Sancta Sanctorum, Rome. Syrian (?), 8th century. Museo Sacro, Vatican. In five colours. Two medallions have survived. The Nativity (plate 51) originally belonged with it. The palmettes between the circles provide the clearest indication of the persistence of Sassanian influence. Otherwise, however, the band is very similar in style to the silks thought to come from Syria, of which the Samson material (plate 48) is a typical example. Perhaps it is the cloth that, according to the *Liber Pontificalis,* was presented to Leo III (795–876): *'rotar siricas, habentes storias Adnuntiatione seu Natale Domini N. J. Christ.'*

53–54.   Lozenge pattern with leaves arranged in the shape of a cross, and the monogram of the Emperor Heraclius (610–641). Silk serge. Very fragmented. From the Madelbert shrine in Liège. Byzantine, 7th century. Musée Diocésan, Liège, as well as in Marburg, Düsseldorf and in the Museo Sacro in the Vatican. This was a very popular costume fabric pattern, as is made clear by mosaics.

55.   Medallion with an emperor on a lion-hunt. Pieces are missing from the top and both sides. Calamanco. Height 73·5 cm. From St Calmin in Mozac (Puy-de-Dôme), formerly in the tomb of St Austremoine; donated to Mozac by Pippin the Short in 761. Byzantine, 8th century. Musée Historique des Tissus, Lyons. The emperor's costume, with its many bright appliqué panels, shows the influence of Sassanian court dress, which also became fashionable in Byzantium. There is a related fragment in Gandersheim, very similar in technique to St Victor's sudarium in Sens with its design of a man strangling a lion. Knowing when the material was donated by the king, we can fix an approximate date of origin.

55. Medallion with the emperor on a lion-hunt.

reminiscent of Syrian textiles like the hippogryph fabric from the Sancta Sanctorum and the horseman fabrics from Milan, Prague and St Calais, as well as of the horse material in Trier and the griffons in St Ursula's, Cologne.

The design on St Victor's sudarium (1·60 m. long) in Sens is of a man (Daniel?) fighting two lions, one on either side of him. It is still completely in the spirit of the Persian Gilgamesh epic. Compared with those we have just dealt with, this material seems earlier and more primitive, but its decoration and place of discovery suggest that it too was probably an 8th-century Byzantine copy. It was in fact found in the reliquary of St Victor, who was martyred in 750, and whose body was brought by Bishop Villicarius from St Maurice d'Agaune to Sens in 759. Taking it to represent Daniel, the weaver copied the design on an earlier silk in Eichstätt.

Closely related to it is the elephant-slayer in the Dumbarton Oaks Collection in Washington (plate 58), though the design here is more mannered. The material is silk: yellow on a dark blue ground with the design in white. Though possibly somewhat later than the Sens sudarium, it goes back to the same source, particularly in its subject-matter. Only the upper part of the panel has survived.

In one variant of the hunting-scene motif the huntsman uses a bow and arrow against the lions. Though they have quite evidently been translated into the Byzantine idiom, like the quadriga material in Aachen and Paris, these cloths are also related to the horseman fabrics of the 'Syrian' group—for example the Maastricht material and the Säckingen Amazon fabric. A little more primitive in style is the tiger cloth from Münsterbilsen now in Brussels, which like the quadriga fabric was found in the Landrada shrine in Brussels. These silk twills were used in a number of places: in St Calais (Sarthe) as a reliquary cloth for the head of St Calais; in the consul library in Prague from 1171 onwards; and on the Wolvinius altar in Sant' Ambrogio in Milan. The large horseman fabric from the shrine of St Cunibert in Cologne (diocesan museum), though related to these, is richer in colour.

On the other hand, the material from Maastricht now in the Victoria and Albert Museum is less complex. The design possibly represents King Bahram V Gor (420–438), who killed a lion and a wild ass with a single arrow, the cognomen 'Gor' being the word for a wild ass. For a long time these cloths too were thought to be Sassanian; but the designs and the colours differ from the Sancta Sanctorum hunting-scene fabrics. Even Falke gave them an early date of origin—around 600—but they must have been later, as their use as an altarcloth in Milan would indicate.

During the course of tracing the development of various individual motifs, we saw that the winged griffon on the Siviard sudarium in Sens represented the zenith of achievement as regards this motif. What had begun as a copy of a Near Eastern original came to have independent validity as a Byzantine work of art. Byzantium reached its political, economic and consequently its cultural peak towards the end of the Macedonian dynasty. When the dynasty came to an end in 1056, Byzantine art lost much of its creative force. Painting aside, what really impresses the world with the splendour of the Byzantine court is its applied art. Enamels like the Limburg cross or the crowns in Budapest, silver reliefs like the women at the sepulchre, ivory reliefs like the reliquary in Cortona (963–969) or the coronation of Romanus in Paris (c. 950), all demonstrate the superiority of these forms of Byzantine art. The same also held true of textiles, particularly silk and cloth-of-gold, which were of such amazing quality that the demand for them was universal. Though the Comnenian dynasty produced some great personalities, for example Alexius I (1048–1118), the decline of the 'second Rome' continued inexorably in politics and art, and it was not long before the recently founded workshops of Palermo, Lucca and Venice were offering serious competition.

Under the Macedonian dynasty countries outside Europe, particularly Abyssinia, continued to influence the imperial workshops of Byzantium. This contact with the Islamic world explains the relative scarcity of Christian themes. An exception to this is the 'Triumph of the Emperor Basil II' which was used in Bamberg as a shroud for Bishop Gunther (died 1065). It is still there, though in a poor state of preservation; the emperor is shown in full regalia riding on a white horse. The bulk of the output of the imperial workshops was made up of silks, generally purple and with designs showing such familiar Near

56. Medallion with a quadriga design. Silk serge. Byzantine, 8th century. Aachen Cathedral treasure.

57. Hippocampi. Silk. Byzantine, 7th century. Musées d'Art et d'Histoire, Brussels.

58. Medallion with elephant-strangler design. Silk serge.
Byzantine, 9th century. Collection Dumbarton Oaks,
Washington.

56. Medallion with a quadriga design. Silk serge. From Charlemagne's tomb in Aachen. Byzantine, 8th century. Aachen Cathedral treasure. Height 76 cm., diameter 66 cm. Another piece of this fabric is now in the Cluny Museum in Paris. The surround is decorated with heart-shaped flowers. On either side of the victorious charioteer is a servant with a whip and a garland. Underneath are two others distributing money (a symbol of generosity) as in Byzantine ivory consular diptychs. The subject is also reminiscent of the charioteer fabric in Brussels (plate 49).

57. Hippocampi. Silk. Byzantine, 7th century. Musées d'Art et d'Histoire, Brussels. Pattern of small contiguous medallions containing confronting hippocampi (the hippocampus being the favourite animal of both Sassanian and Byzantine artists), with polygonal decorative devices at the points of contact. There is another specimen of this type of cloth in the Victoria and Albert Museum in London.

58. Medallion with elephant-strangler design; very fragmented. Silk serge. Byzantine, 9th century. Collection Dumbarton Oaks, Washington. The bottom half has been lost. This piece has much in common with the lion-strangler on St Victor's sudarium in Sens, but it is noticeably more mannered. This can be attributed to the influence of Islamic art. The motif itself is considerably older, occurring as it does in the art of ancient Babylon.

59. Men hunting wild animals. Silk serge. Fragment. The upper medallion is complete, but only a quarter of the lower one has survived. From a reliquary in the Sancta Sanctorum. Byzantine (?), 8th century. Museo Sacro, Vatican. On either side of the Tree of Life two huntsmen are attacking animals with spears: the one above, a lion; the one below, a leopard. They wear green tunics with orbiculi and clavi. This motif is derived from Sassanian art, but is also frequently met with in mosaic floors in Palestine and Syria.

59.   Men hunting wild animals.

60.   Winged horses. Silk serge. Fragment. Part of the upper row has been cut off. Length 21·2 cm. Formerly in the treasure of the Sancta Sanctorum, where it was used as a cushion for the enamel cross of Pope Paschal (817–824). Byzantine, 8th century. Museo Sacro, Vatican. In the upper row four horses step out towards the left, in the lower row to the right. This 'Pegasus' was still exactly the same type of animal as the Sassanian original, which may be seen on silk fabrics from Antinoë which are now in Lyons and Berlin. The high degree of stylisation proves that it was made in Byzantium.

61–62.   A hippocampus and an elephant. Silk serge. Details of a large piece of material decorated with hippocampi (sen-murv), elephants and winged horses in contiguous medallions. Spanish, 11th century. Museo Nazionale del Bargello, Florence. Though this fabric uses all the favourite animal motifs of Sassanian art, it may still be a copy of a Byzantine piece. The elephant motif should be compared with the famous material from Charlemagne's tomb in Aachen, and the winged horses with the fabric in the Vatican. There are other fragments of this cloth in Berlin, in the Museo d'Arte Moderna in Barcelona and in the Cooper Union Museum in New York.

63.   Eagles. Purple silk serge. Fragment. Height 1·60 cm.; eagle 75 cm. Byzantine, c. 1000. The sudarium of St Germain. St Eusèbe, Auxerre. One of the most beautiful examples of the type of imperial eagle, which was also used to decorate the emperor's reception rooms. It is very similar to the design on the chasuble in Bressanone (plate 64). Double-headed eagles were also popular. There are examples of these in Vich, Berlin, Paris and in the Abegg Foundation in Berne.

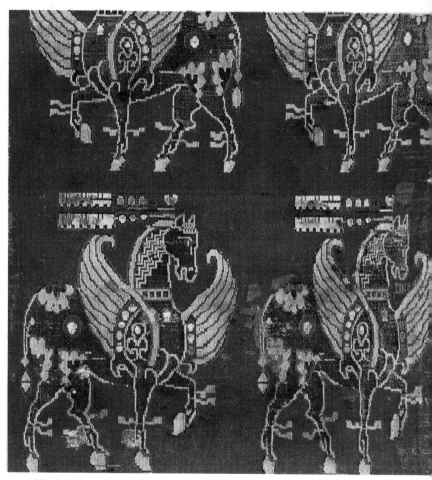

60. Winged horses.

61. Hippocampus. Silk serge; detail of a large piece of
material. Spanish, 11th century. Museo Nazionale del
Bargello, Florence.

62. Elephant. Silk serge; detail of a large piece of material.
Spanish, 11th century. Museo Nazionale del Bargello,
Florence.

63. Eagles. Silk serge. Purple. Fragment. Byzantine, *c*. 1000.
St Eusèbe, Auxerre.

Eastern symbols of power as the imperial eagle, the lion and the elephant. So skilful were the Byzantine artists in adapting the style of these heraldic animals that they remained worthy models until recent times. Otto III laid the wonderful and famous elephant fabric in the tomb of Charlemagne in about the year 1000.

The very size of these materials makes an immediate impression, and the importance given to them in Byzantium is shown by the fact that the name of the workshop in which each one was made was carefully inscribed. Unfortunately one of the most important of them, a lion fabric in Auxerre inscribed with the name of an Emperor Leo (probably Leo VI, 886–912), was lost long ago. And the wonderful purple fabric (2·30 m. long) from St Anno's shrine in Siegburg was destroyed in the last war. It had six lions (75 cm. long) on a purple ground, with the names of Romanus I Lecapenus and his son Christopher (921–931) inscribed between each pair. Of another lion fabric from Deutz with the names of Basil II (976–1025) and Constantine VII and a design of two confronting lions in profile only fragments have survived in Berlin, Düsseldorf, Krefeld and (the largest) Cologne Cathedral. It is a little later than the Siegburg material and differs from it by virtue of its simpler, more monumental style.

Smaller versions of the lion fabric continued to be produced for some considerable time: the one in St Servatius in Maastricht is an excellent example (plate 47). Here too the Sassanian influence can still be discerned.

Equally grandiose are the large eagle fabrics so often mentioned in written sources; and far more of them have survived. The eagle was another symbol of imperial might and, like the lion, was used as a decorative motif on the throne of the Sassanian kings. It also occurs on Ostrogothic and Visigothic buckles. As late as 1295 the *Liber Pontificalis* still speaks *'de panno imperiali de Romania ad aquilas magnas cum duobus capitibus'*. The eagle motif had by then already reached the European courts of Palermo and Apulia. Eagle fabrics were a favourite imperial gift: Henry II gave one to Basle Cathedral and Bishop Albuin (975–1006) donated one (plate 64) to Bressanone Cathedral. The eagle-embroidered dalmatic in Metz may even have been made in Italy. The pieces mentioned so far are still very simple in style, with the eagles placed next to each other; but in the tablium of St Knut (died 1086) in Odense, they are contained in elaborate circular surrounds.

The ring and pendant devices in the beaks of the eagles on the Bressanone fabric and on the sudarium of St Germanus in Auxerre are rather peculiar; they may simply have been copied from a Sassanian original. Both fabrics appear to have been woven at about the same time; the patterns are almost identical and in fact really differ only in colour. As far as the date is concerned, the note about the material donated by Hugo, Bishop of Châlons (999–1039), *'casula purpurea, quae grandes aquilas coloris coccinei contextas circumquaque monstrabant'*, may well refer to the one in Auxerre. There were also double-headed eagles, like those on a purple silk fabric from the reliquary of St Bernardo Calvo (1233–1245). This fabric, of which there are pieces in Vich, Paris and Berlin, is somewhat older, and was probably woven at much the same time as the specimens in Auxerre and Bressanone.

Among the best preserved of these imperial fabrics is the one with the elephant design in Aachen. It was found in the shrine containing the relics of Charlemagne; the Emperor Otto III had spread it over Charlemagne's body in the year 1000. The material is virtually undamaged, and the colours are almost as new (1·62 m. high, 1·36 m. wide). Each of the large contiguous medallions contains an elephant and a stylised tree on a purple ground. The animals carry rich saddle cloths and trappings, and the branches of the trees end in palmettes of the Sassanian type. The areas between the medallions are filled with rosettes. A Greek inscription on the border gives an approximate date: 'Petros Archon of Zeuxippos was deputy to Michael the Chamberlain and keeper of the privy purse.' Since the title of the keeper of the privy purse does not appear before the end of the 9th century, the material must have been woven after the death of Charlemagne. The inscription also indicates that it was a product of the imperial workshop in Zeuxippos. Epimachon, or Epi Michael, was an official, but absolutely nothing is known about Petros Archon.

The anatomy of the animal is still completely Sassanian: it·has lion's paws, a tassel-like tail, and a saddle cloth like similar elephants in Berlin and Siegburg. (This particular fabric came from Spain.)

But the palmette decoration of the surrounds has been adapted to the Byzantine style, as in the Siviard sudarium in Sens. This again indicates that the cloth must have been woven after the death of Charlemagne, in spite of the fact that the *Liber Pontificalis* records, under Leo III, the gift of a fabric '*de fundato cum historia de elephantis*'. Another elephant fabric, from St Josse-sur-Mer (Pas de Calais), now in the Louvre, was produced somewhere in the Islamic world towards the end of the 10th century. The technical quality of the cloth is amazing—something never equalled before or since. If a comparison is made between smaller fabrics of the period (the one with horses in Trier, the one with a panther in Augsburg, or even the one with the bison in Maastricht) and elephant fabrics, it becomes apparent that the designs on these other cloths are less exact and that the various distances that should be equal are in fact often irregular.

The large material from St Julian in Rimini (plate 66) can also be included under the general heading of imperial elephant and lion fabrics. Here too single lions face each other in circular surrounds decorated, as in Sassanian fabrics, with discs. The shape of the animals is very stylised, which brings to mind the griffon fabric in Le Monastier; but the material is equally reminiscent of such imperial lion fabrics as the small Maastricht specimen, even though the stylisation has not gone quite so far. There is also considerable similarity to later Italian brocades, for instance the one from a tomb in Lucca which used to be in the church treasure of St Mary's in Danzig.

64. Chasuble of purple silk serge. Supposed to have
belonged to Bishop Ermanno (1140–1164). Museo
Diocesano, Bressanone.

65. Griffon. Fragment from a reliquary. Silk serge. Byzantine, 10th–11th century. Church treasure, Maastricht.

66. Lions. Purple silk serge. Byzantine, 9th–10th century.
Museo Nazionale, Ravenna.

64.   Chasuble of purple silk serge. Eagle design (*c.* 70 cm. high), cut in places. Said to have belonged to Bishop Ermanno (1140–1164). Museo Diocesano, Bressanone. Its only material difference from the Auxerre eagles (plate 63) is in its colour; it is also worth comparing it with the Vich and Odense eagle fabrics. Like the lion fabric in Cologne and the elephant fabric in Aachen, it was produced by the imperial workshops. It was made a little later than the Metz chasuble with the same motif.

65.   Griffon. Only the protome of the animal has survived. Fragment from a reliquary. Silk serge. Spanish, 10th–11th century. Church treasure, Maastricht. Connected with the large lion fabrics in Cologne and Siegburg and the winged lion material in Amsterdam. Probably made in Byzantium.

66.   Lions. Purple silk serge. From the tomb of St Julian in Rimini. Byzantine, 9th–10th century. Museo Nazionale, Ravenna. Six medallions with lions facing each other. Based on a Sassanian original, but very stylised; they anticipate the large imperial lion fabrics like those in Cologne. This pattern is also used in painting, for example in the frescoes in S. Maria infra portas in Foligno. Somewhat reminiscent of the Maastricht lion pattern.

67.   Two lions. Silk serge. Fragment. The bottom half and parts of the surround on both left and right are missing. From the Sancta Sanctorum. Byzantine, 9th–10th century. Museo Sacro, Vatican. Within the surround are two lions with their heads turned towards each other, one on either side of the Tree of Life *(Haoma)*. The motif is an ancient Middle Eastern one, but the style has been changed, as in the silk fabric with the tiger design from Münsterbilsen, now in Brussels. The other medallions probably contained mythical creatures.

67. Two lions. Fragment. Silk serge. Byzantine, 9th–10th century. Museo Sacro, Vatican.

The new dynasty, that of the Comneni, encouraged silk production as much as their predecessors, and there was no easing of the demand for Byzantine fabrics in the Western world. German church treasures not only comprise the richest store of fabrics from the Macedonian period but also contain numerous materials dating from the Comnenian dynasty. These precious fabrics were also prized in England, and some were imported in 1178. There is a reference to them in the inventory of St Paul's Cathedral for the year 1295, and it has also been pointed out that King John wore Byzantine clothes.

Under the Macedonian dynasty the production of these fabrics had spread to Greece, where Corinth and Thebes became the great centres. Then it spread to Cyprus, where the Byzantine style was adapted *in toto,* despite the fact that the island had been an independent Crusader stronghold since 1192. '*Panni cyprenses*', and particularly gold thread, were exported from Famagusta—usually to Italy, where they were in great demand. Textiles from Cyprus are mentioned in Roman inventories about 1295 and the wonderful materials sent (*c.* 1300) by the great Pope Boniface VIII Caetani to Anagni are still there.

Venice was increasingly threatened by the Seljuks in Asia Minor and the Normans in Sicily, but in 1082 the Venetians signed a treaty with Alexius I Comnenus which gave them commercial equality with the Byzantines. This meant that Venetian merchants no longer had to pay a tariff and that they had complete freedom of residence in Constantinople. As a result, the manufacture of silk cloth moved further west and the Byzantine monopoly was broken, though it of course took the Italians some time to learn the tricks of the trade. In Constantinople itself a peculiar situation existed: the workshops were strongly influenced by Islamic textiles yet Islamic rulers continued to want Byzantine materials. In 1195, for example, the Sultan of Konya begged Alexis III for 40 imperial silk costumes.

The clothes worn by people in mosaics, enamels and miniatures tended to be simply decorated; large figural patterns, especially of animals in circular surrounds, were much rarer. The Grand Admiral Apokandos (c. 1342), for example, wore a blue costume with winged griffons on it. Fabrics with figural designs were probably used for wall-hangings and curtains more than for clothing.

Animal motifs did not change much in style. The old designs borrowed from the Near East as early as the 6th century, particularly lions, griffons, winged horses and various types of birds, generally two in each surround, continued to be used. But geometrical patterns, based on palmettes for example, were becoming much more fashionable. A preference was shown for single colours, and, as a result, delicate intermediate tones gradually disappeared. Several of the animal patterns are so much in the old style that some of them are given a date of origin as early as the 10th century, whereas others, like the lion fabric from the Sancta Sanctorum in the Vatican are thought to be more recent (von Falke suggested it was 13th-century). Some lion fabrics seem more recent still, and the brocade from Halberstadt, now in Berlin, could even be a copy from the Regensburg workshop. It is closer to the material in London (Kendrick no. 1025). The London material is itself more developed and has more movement than the tiger fabric from Munsterbilsen now in Brussels. Perhaps there were also other animal designs, like griffons and birds, on the Sancta Sanctorum fabric—as there were on the London damask.

An approximate date has been given to a wonderful material, specimens of which are in Sion (plate 69) and Berlin. It has a fifty per cent silk warp, a design of two griffons back-to-back, and is almost the exact counterpart of the Aachen elephant fabric. It may be a little later than the Aachen material (as comparison with the almost classically calm griffons on the Siviard sudarium in Sens suggests), but it is not as mannered as another griffon design in Berlin which may have been made as late as the 12th century. Near-Eastern Islamic influence is particularly apparent here, just as it is in glazed ceramics of the same period from Constantinople and Thessalonica.

Two-coloured silks were especially popular in Germany with the Ottos and the princes of the Church. A whole mass of them have survived in church treasures like those of Hildesheim, Brauweiler, Bamberg and Mainz. As a result there is a fairly good chance of dating them. The following fragments of clothing are known: those belonging to Otto I (died 973) in Merseburg; to Henry (died 1024) and his wife Kunigunde in Bamberg Cathedral; to Bishop Willigis (died 1011) in Mainz (plate 70) and Aschaffenburg (the latter fragment is now in the museum in Munich); to Gotthard in Niederaltaich; and to Bernhard in Hildesheim. Finally there are three stoles: one in Brauweiler, which is said to be associated with St Bernard of Clairvaux, and the others in Sugsburg and Regensburg which used to belong to St Ulrich and St Wolfgang respectively.

This type of cloth was used for the imperial cloak in the Hofburg in Vienna and also the marriage cloak (1031) of King Stephen of Hungary, which is richly worked with gold thread. Many of these silks were used for vestments: dalmatics, tablia and stockings. They are a monochrome pale grey, greenish-yellow, red, green or blue-black, with textured designs and a characteristic shimmer like that of satin. The complicated patterns are similar to those on the multi-coloured fabrics: palmettes, rosettes, acanthus leaves, flowers and contiguous medallions. Only St Ulrich's stole has a design showing an emperor. Though abstract in form, these motifs show clear evidence of Eastern influence. Whatever their merits, however, these silk damask-like fabrics do not warrant further study since they were apparently no longer produced after the first half of the 11th century.

Similar but less complicated silks with textured designs using the same motifs continued to be produced in the 12th century. Griffons, birds with wings spread as in the Brauweiler material (plate 71), panthers, lions (heads turned away from each other

68. Pillow and sudarium of St Remigius. Silk twill.
Byzantine (or Persian), 8th–9th century. St Remi, Rheims
69. Two griffons. Silk serge and wool. Fragment; from a
reliquary. Byzantine, 11th century. Musée de Valère, Sion

68. Pillow and sudarium of St Remigius. Senmurv design. Silk twill. Byzantine (or Persian), 8th–9th century. St Remi, Rheims. The Sudarium was placed by Bishop Hincmar of Rheims over the body of St Remigius (died 533) when it was moved to the newly-built church (852). The pillow, as the embroidery on the border informs us, was made by Princess Anpais, at the bishop's request. The design of the senmurv is almost identical to that of the London hippocampi (plate 21).

69. Two griffons back-to-back. Silk serge and wool. Fragment; from a reliquary. Byzantine, 11th century. Musée de Valère, Sion. Three medallions: two complete, the one on the left partly destroyed. Still reminiscent of the winged griffon on the Siviard sudarium in Sens, though later and somewhat coarser. The pontifical stockings from the grave of Pope Clement II (died 1047) in Bamberg Cathedral provide another example of this type of fabric (now in Berlin). The heart-shaped palmettes of the circular surrounds are the clearest indication that this material came from Byzantium.

70. The chasuble of Bishop Willigis (975–1011). Slashed silk, compound twill; with decorative motifs. Byzantine, 11th century. Cathedral museum, Mainz. Two different forms of palmette in pointed oval surrounds. Its attribution to Bishop Willigis of Mainz, and the date given to the material as a consequence, are supported by a whole succession of similar slashed silks belonging to Ottonian rulers and princes of the church (Otto I's in Merseburg, Clement II's (died 1047) in Bamberg, St Heribert's (999–1021) in Deutz, St Ulrich's (died 973) in Augsburg, St Berward's (died 1022) in Hildesheim). The liveliness of the decoration anticipates the Byzantine fabrics of the 11th century which, though monochrome, have elaborate textural patterns.

71. Two birds. From a chasuble in Brauweiler. Slashed silk lampas. Byzantine, 11th century. St Nicholas, Brauweiler. Monochrome. Each medallion contains two birds, one on each side of a Tree of Life. The chasuble (1·37 m. long) has a gold border. Legend has it that this is the chasuble worn by Bernard of Clairvaux when he called for a crusade in Brauweiler (1147). Though older, the material is close to monochrome slashed materials like Ulrich's chasuble in Augsburg. They draw their inspiration from Sassanian and Islamic originals respectively.

70.　Chasuble of Bishop Willigis (975–1011).

71. Two birds. Slashed silk lampas. Byzantine, 11th century,
St Nicholas, Brauweiler.

or standing on either side of the Tree of Life), all usually in decorated surrounds, occur quite frequently. Ornamentation, however, became increasingly rigid and formal, though even in the 12th century these silks retained something of their former grace.

Surprisingly enough, Byzantine silks became increasingly rare, and to get some idea of what was being worn in the last centuries of the empire it is essential to study the portraits, and particularly the miniatures, of important political and clerical figures. One of the most popular designs among people of this class was a pattern of palmettes running through the whole material. Good examples of this can be seen on the chasubles of Willigis in Mainz Cathedral (plate 70) and of Ulrich in Augsburg.

The Palaeologue era (1261–1453) witnessed a further degeneration in these motifs. Furthermore, the art of embroidery began to be developed, first in Constantinople and subsequently in other lands. Although the technique of embroidery had been known and admired in Constantinople since the earliest times, it was only in this late period that it was employed to an enormous degree, especially for clerical vestments. A number of important specimens of these have survived: the epitaphios (Byzantine Museum, Athens) from Thessalonica or Ochrid, a gift from Andronicus II Palaeologus (1282–1328); and Charlemagne's dalmatic in St Peter's, Rome, with Christ and the angels on one side of it and the Transfiguration on the other (probably 14th-century work).

Two items from Castell'Arquato (14th century) with a Last Supper design display the style favoured under the Palaeologi. A date around 1208 has been given to two other fabrics, showing Jesus and Mary, from the grave of Philip of Swabia in Speyer Cathedral; they are now in the Bavarian National Museum in Munich. Photius's *sakkos* in Moscow already exemplifies the more ornamental style of the 15th century.

As well as large churches, monasteries, like Mount Athos or Meteora in Greece, Sagorsk near Moscow, Rila in Bulgaria, Putva in Roumania, managed to preserve a considerable number of these precious embroidered fabrics of the post-Byzantine period. The love of colourful stuffs, which is still apparent in the folk art of these countries, is part of their Byzantine heritage.

LIST OF ILLUSTRATIONS   Page

Wool on linen. Egyptian, 4th century. Collection E. Kofler-Truniger, Lucerne.